GOOD TIME GIRLS of COLORADO

A Red-Light History of the Centennial State

Jan MacKell Collins

TWODOT®

GUILFORD, CONNECTICUT
HELENA, MONTANA

A · TWODOT® · BOOK

An imprint and registered trademark of
The Rowman & Littlefield Publishing Group, Inc.
4501 Forbes Blvd., Ste. 200
Lanham, MD 20706
www.rowman.com

Distributed by NATIONAL BOOK NETWORK

British Library Cataloguing in Publication Information Available

Library of Congress Cataloging-in-Publication Data Available

ISBN 978-1-4930-3805-3 (paperback)
ISBN 978-1-4930-3806-0 (e-book)

∞™ The paper used in this publication meets the minimum requirements of American National Standard for Information Sciences—Permanence of Paper for Printed Library Materials, ANSI/NISO Z39.48-1992.

Printed in the United States of America

CONTENTS

CONTENTS

ACKNOWLEDGMENTS

———•●•———

It is no secret to my many friends and colleagues in Colorado, which I haunted from the early 1960s, that I am fascinated with the history of that state's good time girls. The list of those I need to thank for their time, patience, information, and resources seems simply innumerable. Some of them are no longer with us, and I continue making new friends in the history realm even today. I can't possibly eliminate any of these people from this list, but I will try to at least tone it down.

My research all began in Colorado Springs. The late Mary Davis and Cal Otto, as well as their wonderful staff at Penrose Library in Colorado Springs, not only provided me with some great information, but also gave me a wealth of opportunities that included an appearance on Rocky Mountain PBS. The late Leland Feitz and Paul Idleman of the Old Colorado City Historical Society provided much encouragement and insight. Dianne Hartshorn has not only kept the memory of madam Blanche Burton alive, but has also been of great help and support to me. Thayer Tutt of the El Pomar Foundation has been marvelous at putting up with me occasionally making him blush with stories of the red-light ladies in the early days. Farther south, in Pueblo, it was my pleasure to finally connect with historian Joanne West Dodds, and I appreciate the effort she put forth in assisting me with additional research.

The Cripple Creek District, where I lived for many years, remains in the top tier of my favorite places. Madams Charlotte Bumgarner, Lodi Hern, and the other ladies of the Old Homestead museum have always been supportive of my work, including those few years I was able to manage this most authentic and historic brothel museum. My dear friend Georganna Peiffer has always supported and encouraged me in her gentle way. Erik Swanson, former director of the Cripple Creek District Museum, as well as museum founder Richard Johnson, gave me a job there and spent countless hours counseling me in my work and my research. Thanks also go to the late Ohrt Yeager and Steve Mackin, the late Sally Johnson, and Sally's daughter, Paula Waddington, for allowing me to interview them and providing amazing information about "French Blanche" LaCroix. La Jean Greeson, my friend in faraway Washington, is a research goddess. Crystal Brown, Lisa Wheatcraft, and Linda Weidman at the Teller County Courthouse in Cripple Creek have been of immense help.

Melissa Trenary, my sometime "partner in crime," remains my best friend who is always up for an adventure or a new idea and worked with me for many years at the Cripple Creek District Museum. Michael Duffy and Rick Leonard of the fabulous and historic Cripple Creek Hospitality House (formerly the Teller County Hospital) have also been supportive of my research on French Blanche. Terri Hubert, Dickie Grater, Kim Tulley, Ruth Zirkle, Sherry Skye Johns, Mary Sanders, Lori Sewald, and Mark Gregory—plus so many, many more—all encouraged me, told me stories, and read my books. Thank you also to former Victor resident and history author Cathleen Norman, who once looked at my nervous face before a presentation in Arizona, sighed, and reminded me, "You know the material. You can do this."

In Denver, it was University of Colorado history professor and state historian Dr. Tom Noel who first encouraged me to give a presentation about the bad girls of Colorado and consequently enabled me to publish my first book, *Brothels, Bordellos & Bad Girls: Prostitution in Colorado 1860–1930*. Tom is better known as "Dr. Colorado" in certain circles and gives wonderful walking tours, great cheer, and excellent advice. I cannot say enough good things about the staff of the Denver Public Library and Stephen H. Hart Library, nor the wonderful staff of History Colorado, all of whom so carefully tend to their historic collections. Thank you too to all of the wonderful strangers I have encountered in libraries and museums in Boulder, Central City, Durango, Oak Creek, Ouray, Silverton, Telluride, and other places throughout the state who helped me find what I was looking for. And to the all of the people who have bought my books, attended my presentations, followed me on social media, and listened to me babble endlessly about my giddy girls, I raise my glass to you. I could not have done all of this without each of you.

When you write about hookers and harlots for a very long time, you sometimes get your wires crossed. I am indebted to Erin Turner, Alex Bordelon, and others at Globe Pequot Press for their assistance in weeding through my manuscript, sources, and footnotes to make sure I got everything correct and in place. Because of their diligence, the book makes sense and does not sound like me when I am babbling history at someone in conversation. Thank you, everybody.

On a more personal note, I wish my mother and mentor, Eleanor Smith, was still around to see how far my books have come. She will always remain in my heart as my best friend and number one fan. Other family fans who have encouraged and supported me through time include my niece, Dawn Santabanez; my dad, Wally Smith; my stepmother, Barbara Espino; my patient husband, Corey; and my godmother, Irene Smith, who loved looking me in the eye and declaring with a grin, "So, you want to be a writer, eh?"

INTRODUCTION

———◦●●◦———

Colorado's Mile-High Maidens

Colorado is one of the most beautiful states in America. Here, majestic mountain peaks can tower over fourteen thousand feet. High mountain meadows, flat and colorful grasslands, and beautiful prairies sprawl below them. The Rocky Mountains create a great scar that cuts ferociously right down the middle of the state. To the east are high prairies and agriculture; to the west are monumental mountains and mining. From any point in the state, stellar mountain ranges loom under blue summer skies or over winter blankets of snow, sometimes both. These wild landscapes can resemble heaven on Earth. Or, they can be jagged and unforgiving places where one wrong step can mean death. This has been Colorado since the beginning of time. From a distance, it is not at all hard to see the same Colorado that the first Anglo explorers viewed when they came west.

Colorado's heritage dates back centuries. Native Americans found much of the state a haven for hunting, fishing, gathering food, and creating comfortable living conditions for much of the year. Beginning in the 1600s, the southern portion of the state was visited by Mexican and Spanish explorers. All three of these peoples, with their separate ways of living and their ideals of culture, battled it out over territories for centuries. Add the French fur trappers of the early nineteenth century and the miners of the 1850s, and here is a most unique blend of early pioneers who recognized and utilized Colorado's resources in a vast, untamed land. They may not have agreed but upon one thing: Colorado offers a stunning landscape and an amazing way of life, if one knows how to do it right.

Captain William Becknell, the "Father of the Santa Fe Trail," and his party first set out for Santa Fe from Franklin, Missouri, in September 1821. Within a short time, two main routes were accessed. The shorter trail was the Cimarron Cutoff at Cimarron, Kansas, which took travelers through Oklahoma and only a tiny portion of Colorado before rejoining the original trail near Watrous, New Mexico. The longer trail was the Mountain Branch, which continued directly west into Colorado, stopping at Bent's Fort and later Pueblo before turning south to Trinidad and into New Mexico. The Mountain Branch, while not as fast as the Cimarron Cutoff, was considered the easier route for heavier-loaded wagons, and safer. Still, Anglo-American women did not appear along the trail until 1832, when Mary Donoho was recorded as the first Anglo woman to make the trek.[1]

Up until that time, the few women of easy virtue in Colorado consisted exclusively of Mexicans, Spaniards, and Native Americans, many of whom were born and raised there. When Colorado finally experienced its first gold boom during the late 1850s, prospectors by the thousands flocked to the state. These hardy fortune seekers had hardly swung a pickax before Anglo prostitutes also saw a gold mine that could yield wealth: the men themselves. Proper women would follow later, traipsing after their husbands or at least looking for one. For a few short years, however, the pioneer harlots had their fair pick of men from whose pockets might flow gold, silver, and cash.

The gay ladies who tramped their way into Colorado during its formative years were an interesting and sturdy bunch. In the first decade of Colorado's gold rush, anyone wishing to access the Centennial State did so by horseback, wagon, or stagecoach. Some trails from Kansas, New Mexico, and Wyoming were well traveled, while others were no more than ancient paths used by Native Americans for centuries. All could prove treacherous; before it came under use by the Butterfield Stage Line, the Smoky Hill Trail between Atchison, Kansas, and Denver was alternately known as the "Starvation Trail."[2] Not until 1867 was the first railroad, the Denver Pacific Railway & Telegraph Company, established. The line ran between Denver and Cheyenne, Wyoming, hooking up with the Union Pacific Railroad. Still, the tracks spanning the hundred-mile distance between the two towns would not open for service until 1870.

Men may have lusted for gold, but the lack of female companionship in the early days could prove difficult for them. After a hard day's work, or week, or at payday, the boys naturally wanted to blow off some steam. Dances were a favorite pastime, but nearly always lacked female partners. In these instances, men attending such events designated "female" dance partners by tying ribbons or handkerchiefs on their arms. On those rare occasions that a woman attended a dance, she could rely on being treated with respect but was expected to dance with anyone who asked. The few married men who brought their wives were obligated by social standards of the day to allow them to dance with others.

Denver's very first "white" prostitute was said to be Ada LaMont, a nineteen-year-old beauty who married a young minister and came west with him in about 1858. Midway through the trip the minister disappeared, allegedly along with a young lady of questionable character. Ada arrived in Denver alone—but with a whole new outlook on her situation. "As of tomorrow," she said, "I start the first brothel in this settlement."[3] At the time, only about 1 percent of the few women in Colorado practiced prostitution. In 1859 Libeus Barney observed, "There are few ladies [in Denver] yet, but there are females of questionable morality about town."[4] Those prostitutes who made it as far as

Denver eventually began drifting off to the mining camps west of town. In Georgia Gulch near Breckenridge, a group of miners got word that a woman was in town and serving drinks at a local saloon. The men fairly rushed to the tavern like "boys who go to see a monkey."[5]

Not all barmaids, nor prostitutes, were welcome; in 1859 a fledgling bordello in Nevadaville, located above Central City, was closed down by its Bible-thumping population and the naughty ladies were chased out of town. A more sympathetic ear was given to one young woman who told others in 1860 that her career in the industry began in St. Louis. At the tender age of fifteen, she said, she made the mistake of running off with a "gay and dashing city youth." The man took her to his aunt's house, where she was given drugs and wine. "When I awoke to consciousness at about noon of the next day," she explained, "I found this residence miraculously transformed into a house of shame."[6] These two incidents in particular illustrate the pro and con attitudes the public would take toward the prostitution industry for the next several decades.

Authorities throughout Colorado would eventually introduce a series of ordinances prohibiting prostitution. For many years, however, the industry ran largely unregulated. Only the watchful eyes of certain citizens monitored the sex trade and occasionally tried to do something about it. But when a group of respectable women in Denver suggested taking "fallen" women into private homes as a means of rehabilitating them in 1871, the *Rocky Mountain News* shot down the idea. The practice, the editors maintained, would only "corrupt other women."[7] As for the soiled doves, many found the smaller camps and communities nestled in the Rocky Mountains more welcoming. They were not, however, beyond trying out the blooming metropolises of Colorado City, Denver, Grand Junction, Pueblo, and other places.

By the time Colorado was made a state in 1876, at least a few cities were taking steps toward controlling the skin trade. Early ordinances were limited successes at best. In Fort Collins, city officials made the dire mistake of repealing an ordinance prohibiting saloons, apparently without considering the women who worked in them. Both the tavern owners and the wayward women took full advantage of the act, and gambling dens and saloons soon peppered the downtown area—too many, in fact. The law intervened when possible. During one instance in 1881, four "Negro" girls from a local dance hall pulled up in front of a local saloon. Their fancy buggy was driven by a white man, appalling witnesses who saw the spectacle. When the ladies entered the tavern, the sheriff followed them inside and booted them out. Two years later, the town fathers raised the price of a liquor license from $300 to $1,000 to keep out the riffraff. The plan worked, and the number of saloons soon numbered only six.[8]

Other cities throughout Colorado were experiencing similar issues. In 1879 a local newspaper complained that Georgetown had twelve saloons and parlor houses, but not one school. Indeed, Brownell Street had no fewer than five expensive parlor houses at one time, as well as the usual assortment of smaller brothels, taverns, and gambling halls. Two of Georgetown's more notorious madams were Mattie Estes and Mollie Dean. In typical frontier fashion, Mollie met her death at the hands of a jealous lover after being seen with another man. By then Georgetown was as used to violence as any other western town. Shortly after a miner was shot to death in her brothel, madam Jennie Aiken was killed when the pleasure palace burned to the ground.

Newspapers in general were soon hardened to the violence among red-light women, reporting on their deaths as they would anybody else—if they chose to report on those deaths at all. And when they did, their attitude often reflected that the women got what they deserved. By the 1880s, it was hard not to notice the lurid activities, violence, drunkenness, and other aspects of the unseemly lifestyle led by prostitutes across the state. Newspapers increasingly reported on the bevy of bad girls who had fairly infiltrated every nook and cranny of the mountains and plains. Leadville, for instance, was recorded as having a brothel for every 129 people in town.

The high-altitude camp of Caribou, in Boulder County, was one of the few communities to actually ban gamblers and loose women. The law was surprisingly easy to uphold, perhaps because Caribou was at an elevation of nearly ten thousand feet. The barren landscape was subject to hundred-mile-per-hour winds and suffered terrible snowstorms, with drifts that could top twenty-five feet in height. There being no railroad to Caribou, most prostitutes found it difficult to attract new customers. With the new law in place, most of them simply relocated to the old mining town of Cardinal two miles south. Known alternately as Cardinal City and New Cardinal, the revitalized town was a true "sin city" occupied specifically by saloonkeepers and prostitutes for vices and pleasures of the flesh. The ladies found a larger customer base of men not only from Caribou, but also from the nearby mining towns of Nederland, Blackhawk, and Central City.

As much as they were unwelcome in Colorado on the official front, wanton women did find acceptance in many places throughout the state. Although the dance halls in Lake City rarely closed their doors, an exception was made in April of 1882 after Sheriff E. N. Campbell was killed while staking out a robbery. Notably, the dance halls took the day off out of respect for the fallen lawman. It was not unusual to find policemen who visited and maintained friendships with ladies of the evening. One of the best-known law officers in Gunnison in 1884 was Cyrus "Doc" Shores. It was Shores's duty to keep law and order in town, which included the local red-light district, but he also was friends with Denver prostitute Molly Foley. The 1880s were a prime time for prostitutes in Gunnison, who brazenly entertained right along Main Street near Tomichi Avenue. Men could access the Red-light Dance Hall and Fat Jack's Amusement Palace, plus at least three two-story houses of ill repute. In 1882 two men named Walsh and Yard fought it out over a dance-hall girl named Viola. Walsh was killed, and Yard's trial ended in a hung jury before he was acquitted.

COPYRIGHT 1905
J. TULLY

C-178

An early postcard portrays a delightful little dance-hall girl from the early 1900s.
Courtesy Jan MacKell Collins.

In time, literally hundreds of mining camps, towns, and cities could be found all over Colorado. Ladies of the evening had the divine leisure of traveling from place to place, a common practice to prevent being labeled an "old-timer" in any one town. In 1885 child pioneer Anne Ellis recalled encountering a traveling prostitute camped near the town of Bonanza, Colorado. "We went over to investigate, and found a course [sic], red-faced woman, her straw colored hair hanging in her eyes. She was one who had fallen so low that she drove from one camp to another, plying her trade in these tents." Ellis did note that the woman later married an Englishman and moved into "one of the best houses in town." A visit to her revealed "diamonds, very red plush furniture, and her very pale blue and bright pink tea gowns; also a parrot and a cage of parakeets."[9]

The lady of Bonanza was indeed lucky. Many women in the sex trade aspired to marry and end their careers as prostitutes. Although few were able to do so, there were others who were quite successful at transforming one of their customers into a husband. Colorado pioneer Mary Mathews noted, "Sometimes a good citizen, wealthy and respectable, marries his wife from some of these corrupt houses, and he seldom ever regrets his choice. He builds her up to be respected and respectable. I have heard of several cases."[10]

The sight of disheveled prostitutes was unfortunately common, especially in the more populated towns. In 1886 in Ouray, newspapers reported on a drunken prostitute who was seen "reeling along the sidewalk, scattering school children—on their way from dinner to school—right and left, in her wild flight." At last the girl fell and "wallowed all over the sidewalk" until someone helped her to her feet.[11] Alcohol and drugs were staples of the red-light way of life. In the days before simple aspirin and other modern painkillers, the ailing regularly used stronger drugs. Depression ran high among the girls, many of whom became addicted to such vices to escape their problems. Most standard medicines contained potentially lethal doses of such drugs as morphine, cocaine, opium, or alcohol. Wyeth's New Enterius Pills, Feeley's Rheumatic Mixture, and Godfrey's Cordial all contained morphine. Laudanum, a liquid form of opium, was applied to sprains and bruises or consumed straight from the bottle. Combinations of morphine and cocaine relieved colds. Visiting opium dens in the back of Chinese laundries or brothels was also a popular pastime.

Drunken, slatternly, and downright wicked women were the way prostitutes were regarded by most of the general public. But in a time when the average working woman at a legitimate job made a paltry six dollars per week, a position in the prostitution industry could yield much more. The average trick cost from a quarter to a dollar at a crib, ten dollars in a brothel, and from five to fifty dollars in a fancy parlor house. A good prostitute averaged between four and ten tricks per day. But being a soiled dove required strength, patience, common sense, and even good moral beliefs. Many prostitutes who came from religious backgrounds tended to stay faithful to their respective churches. Shady ladies were known to gather donations for, or contribute to, building churches in the towns in which they lived. A number of them also attended services, if only to sit in the back row and slip out before services ended.

In many communities, prostitutes were publicly banned from churches and deliberately snubbed when they died. In 1900 Jessie Landers lay dying from tuberculosis in Lake City. The girl asked the Reverend M. B. Milne of the Baptist church to conduct services for her. He agreed. When Jessie died, one of the trustees of the church refused to open the doors and admit the funeral party. The services were held elsewhere, with Reverend Milne keeping his promise and even accompanying the mourners to the cemetery. Later, the church trustee who had refused admittance was followed and horsewhipped by two of Jessie's friends. Also in Lake City, the Reverend George Darley of the

Presbyterian church provided services after prostitute Maggie Hartman died of pneumonia. Afterward he even visited her former house of employment and shook hands with each of the girls.

Hypocrisy in government echoed the public's view of the prostitution industry. In time, Colorado passed a number of ordinances against prostitution in various forms. But the industry was a cash cow: Soiled doves were regularly arrested, dragged into court, and fined for violating the law. In time, the fines were paid on a monthly basis, which, although prostitution remained illegal, satisfied the city coffer until the next month. In Frisco in about 1883, the city was suffering financially, to the extent that gaming tables, houses of prostitution, and saloons were ultimately taxed to bring in more money. It was not until 1889 that Colorado passed a law making it illegal to solicit girls under the age of eighteen years to work in a brothel, reducing cities' income. By the early 1900s, paying monthly fines was standard procedure and nearly all cities counted on the money as part of their income. In Silverton, the ladies of the night paid so much to the city for their monthly fines and health exams that local taxes were considerably lower than in other towns in comparison.

In 1915 suffragist and early Colorado state senator Helen Ring Robinson successfully passed a law making houses of prostitution illegal on the basis that they were a nuisance. Such places would be raided, their furnishings sold off, and the house locked up for one year. Only a bond by the property owner, with a statement that the structure would not be used for prostitution again, would allow the locks to come off. Robinson's decree was followed by statewide prohibition as of January 1, 1916. During World War I, intervention by the military further hampered frontier prostitution as it was once known around the West. By World War II, prostitution still had a presence in Colorado, as well as other places throughout America. But it would never again be the same as it once was in the woolly, wild West.

SIN ON THE SANTA FE TRAIL

————◆●◆————

The famed Santa Fe Trail became a gateway to the West for thousands of men beginning in 1821. Due to the perils of traversing
an unknown land fraught with Native Americans, barren lands, questionable water sources, unpredictable weather, and other unknown
risks, women were pretty much forbidden, even among themselves,
from taking on such a journey. Until 1832 no Anglo women of record
traveled the Santa Fe Trail east to Santa Fe, ruling out the possibility of
any prostitutes making the trek.

It was generally known, however, that certain traders along the trail
routinely captured Native Americans and sold them as slaves, sometimes prostitutes. "It was no uncommon thing in those days to see a
party of Mexicans in that country buying Indians," said Richard "Uncle
Dick" Wootten of Raton Pass on the Colorado and New Mexico border,
"and while we were trapping there I sent a lot of peltries to Taos by a
party of those same slave traders."[1] Although Wootten did not point out
the presence of prostitutes in the parties he saw, they were no doubt
among the slaves.

The Mountain Branch of the Santa Fe Trail extended into Colorado,
with better access to shelter in the way of camps, forts, and cities. Beginning with the construction of Bent's Fort along the Arkansas River in
1833, travelers found easier access to water, supplies, and flatter terrain
for those with loaded-down wagons. Trader William Bent and his brothers established the fort as the first trading post west of the Mississippi,
making it a most popular stopping place. Eventually, travelers also could

access a second fort at today's Pueblo before turning south to New Mexico. The Bents were highly respected, and although prostitution was not permitted inside the fort, a handful of women usually plied their trade in close proximity. They were still almost exclusively Mexican, Spanish, and Native American.

By the 1840s women from all walks of life were traveling the Santa Fe Trail. "Camp followers," the euphemism of the day for prostitutes or any other women wandering around without a man, were among them.[2] These adventurous ladies hitched up with wagon trains, military troops, and whoever else would allow them as traveling companions in hopes of making the journey in relative safety. Those who risked going it alone could fall victim to attacks, kidnapping, rape, torture, and death. Therefore, it was wiser for these women to find a group, preferably a larger one where they might easily blend in, to travel with. Safety in numbers was the name of the game, and some women found it quite lucrative to make their way with others of their kind in a caravan or the same wagon. Finding a group of single men or soldiers to hook up with guaranteed not only more safety, but also a way to make money or trade for goods along the way.

One of the very earliest accounts of prostitution in Colorado was documented at the settlement of Greenhorn, twenty-five miles south of Pueblo close to both the Santa Fe and Taos Trails. In 1841 fur trapper John Brown fought a duel with another man over a Mexican flirt known as Nicolasa. The duel took place on the ranch of Jose Weis on the Greenhorn River. During her flighty reign, Nicolasa had already been the cause of two other duels. Brown won, but Nicolasa was nowhere to be found when the ex-trapper set up a trading post at Greenhorn in about 1845. In her stead was Luisa Sandoval, the alleged ex-wife of Jim Beckwourth.

Beckwourth claimed in his autobiography that he married a woman he called Louise Sandeville at Taos in 1842. Shortly afterward, the couple departed for Colorado. Explorer John C. Frémont reported seeing Luisa at a camp along the Platte River a short time later. In 1843 Beckwourth left Luisa and a daughter named Matilda at Pueblo. By the time he returned in 1846, Luisa had married John Brown and the two had settled at Greenhorn. Beckwourth later claimed that Brown had tricked Luisa into marrying him and that she had tried to come back to him but he refused her. Luisa moved to California with her family in 1849, where Brown became a prominent businessman. She never did comment on Beckwourth's claims, possibly because she was once a fallen woman.

When Bent's New Fort was established farther west along the trail after 1849, it was commonly known that sex was for sale in a "raucous and unruly" community located outside the walls of the fort.[3] Bent's New Fort made a great place to linger and trade sex for goods and money while gathering information about what lay ahead. Of his visit there in 1850, Lewis Garrard commented that "the only female women there were Charlotte the cook and Rosalie, half French, half Indian. But they had a dance just the same, and Frenchmen from St. Louis and Canada and backwoodsmen from Missouri swayed to wild music."[4]

As settlers on the Santa Fe Trail increased in number, more and more places became viable stopping points for people traveling the trail. In 1853 James Mead noted that "every trading or hunting establishment was called a ranch" and such places offered a variety of merchandise, as well as water, whiskey, and women.[5] Fellow traveler Robert Peck explained that these places were almost always surrounded by walls or other barriers to protect against Indian attacks. In many instances, working girls were allowed to operate within the confines of certain ranches. After all, the ranchers no doubt profited from a percentage of the money the ladies made.

Still, travel was dangerous in those early years, even as forts and settlements continued to sprout up. When Fort Pueblo was established in 1853, those in outlying communities, as well as travelers, felt better protected from Indian attacks. From the fort, wagon trains could follow the Taos Trail or resume their trip along the Santa Fe. There is little doubt that Mexican and Indian prostitutes operated at Fort Pueblo as Anglo women continued coming west. In time, as Fort Pueblo became a city, the accompanying Anglo red-light districts flourished in today's downtown area for many years.

The "59ers" who came west seeking gold opened up new opportunities as a series of new trails branched off of the Santa Fe. The influx of people was quite amazing, bringing "gold grubbers, town puffers, purring prostitutes, glinty-eyed gamblers and ink smeared journalists."[6] Like generations before them, these folks kept a lookout for Pikes Peak (elevation 14,114 feet), the highest landmark visible from the east. The phrase "Pikes Peak or Bust" was scrawled across many a wagon canvas as prospectors and others scrambled across the prairies, hoping to make their fortune in gold. Although newcomers came from all over America and beyond, a good many of them utilized the Santa Fe Trail.

Trinidad, settled in about 1861 along the Santa Fe as it neared the New Mexico border, also naturally sported numerous shady ladies over time. In 1874 one woman, Moll Howard of Las Animas, was killed with a rock by a man named Spinner. The man claimed that the woman had attacked him with a butcher knife and owed him a dollar besides. When Moll's friends heard about the murder in Las Animas, they formed an angry mob and hanged Spinner at the nearby Purgatoire River. Moll Howard was just one of many wanton women to meet an untimely end in the region.

In 1876 the Denver and Rio Grande Railroad reached the town of El Moro just five miles northeast of Trinidad. Train and stage passengers could now ride to El Moro and continue their journey south on the Santa Fe Trail. Before long there were four bars at El Moro, and George Close kept a dance hall around the corner from the New State Hotel,

For decades Pikes Peak, looming high above the Colorado plains, gave travelers a sense of direction and hope.

Courtesy Jan MacKell Collins.

with its fancy saloon. One of his employees was Jennie Lawrence, lately of Pueblo. One night a drunken Indian called Navajo Frank took a shot at Close. The bullet missed its mark and hit Jennie instead, piercing her heart before passing through the coat sleeve of her dance partner, mildly wounding the fiddler and lodging in a wall.

Plenty of wayward women passed through Trinidad in its day. The most famous of them was Kate Elder, aka Big Nose Kate, who spent time in town with her notorious consort, Doc Holliday. When the couple left Dodge City, Kansas, they probably utilized the new Atchison, Topeka and Santa Fe Railroad to make their way to Trinidad in 1879.[7] Their stay there actually only lasted ten days. The twosome was forced to beat a hasty retreat after Holliday shot a young gambler known as "Kid Colton" over a "trivial matter."[8] Kate and her man moved south to Las Vegas, New Mexico, where the *Las Vegas Optic* later called Holliday "a shiftless, bagged-legged character—a killer and a professional cut-throat and not a wit too refined to rob stages or even steal sheep." Kate, they said, was "a Santa Fe tid-bit and surrounded her habiliments with a detestable odor before leaving the 'ancient' [city] that will in itself make her memory immortal."[9]

In time, Trinidad's red-light districts grew to epic proportions. The first district appeared very near the Santa Fe Trail behind Commercial Street. Fancy parlor houses with dance floors and musical entertainment were eventually constructed on Mill and Plum Streets. Downtown, "bar girls" worked above the taverns along Main Street, and certain restaurants provided curtained booths to keep their customers anonymous while they dined with ladies of the evening. A Romanesque building constructed in 1888 at 115 East Main Street came complete, unbeknownst to the owner, with a bust of a local madam in the front facade. Allegedly, the architect was in love with her.

The best-known prostitute in Trinidad at the turn of the century was Mae Phelps, who in 1900 was at 228 Santa Fe Avenue with ten employees. Mae dressed very regally in smart business suits. Notably, she worked with other local madams to form the Madams' Association, which worked with city officials to run a special trolley system into the red-light district. And in 1927 she allegedly had a hand in establishing the Madam's Rest Home, a quaint four-bedroom home located outside of town on the road to Sopris.

As Trinidad and other towns along the Santa Fe Trail grew, and as railroad traffic increased, fewer and fewer people utilized the old trail. The exception might have been those who simply could not afford a passenger ticket or were on the move with a wagon full of household goods or perhaps even those eluding the law who feared being recognized on the train. Even so, the trail remained a known route as late as 1900, when it was referenced during one of Mae Phelps's court appearances, charging her with prostitution. During her trial, attorney Jamie McKeough asked Mae if she "operated a public place on the Santa Fe Trail." In answer Mae quipped, "You ought to know, you've been there often enough."[10]

LADIES OF THE CAMPS

---◗●◗---

By 1858, Colorado was in the beginning stages of its first mining boom. Colorado Territory would be created three years later, using sections of Kansas, Nebraska, New Mexico, and Utah territories. "Pikes Peak or Bust" was the popular motto of the day as prospectors by the thousands flocked to the new territory. They came on foot, by horseback, or in wagons—any means to reach a new frontier which might yield riches beyond a man's wildest dreams. The pioneers bravely ventured into the Rocky Mountains, scaling their craggy faces and weathering harsh winters while setting up meager camps. Within these forlorn places, they had no choice but to scramble for food, shelter, and water or risk dying of starvation or hypothermia.

Many of the men who came to Colorado were able to scrape out a living to some degree. Some became rich. Some gave up mining and found other ways to make money as doctors, lawyers, merchants, teamsters, blacksmiths, and other professions. Of the few women who made the trek over the trails to Colorado, at least some of them were prostitutes bent on earning their own way by selling entertainment, and sex, to the men.

Although travelers coming west used Pikes Peak as their guide into Colorado, the earliest gold diggings were actually west of Denver. Women were initially so scarce in the fledgling town that the "mere mention of a bonnet on the streets of Denver in 1859 brought Argonauts bolting to their doors, and a youth in another Colorado mining camp paid twenty dollars in gold dust for the initial pancake made by the region's first unmarried woman."[1] By 1860 prostitution was prominent in places like Golden City, where correspondent Albert D. Richardson spent some time during July. Richardson sent letters to the publisher of the *Lawrence Republican* in Kansas, which duly published the writer's adventures and observations of the gold boom in full swing. On one occasion, Richardson reported that a soldier stole "$175, three gold watches, and $200 worth of jewelry from a house of prostitution. On pursuing and overtaking the regiment, the disconsolate proprietor found that the thieves had deserted, taking eighteen horses with them, and that twenty dragoons had gone in pursuit."[2]

Prospectors heading to Colorado soon branched out all over the state. Buckskin Joe, located at the bottom of Mosquito Pass outside of Alma, was among the earliest Colorado towns to generate tales of dance hall dames and loose women. Founded in 1861 as Laurette and changed to Buckskin Joe in 1865, the camp's population soon included fifty women "from all walks of life." There was also a "fairly extensive" red-light district on the edge of town.[3] In addition to doing business in Buckskin Joe, the ladies could travel over relatively short distances to other budding camps, or even cross precarious Mosquito Pass (altitude 13,186 feet) over to Leadville and conduct their business there. Here too was Colorado's earliest red-light legend, Silver Heels. A dance-hall girl with silver heels on the bottom of her slippers, Silver Heels was caught up in a smallpox epidemic, during which she nursed the sick before catching the dreaded disease herself. Scarred for life, Silver Heels left town. Years later, a woman bearing her likeness was seen walking among the tombstones at the local cemetery, a veil covering her disfigured face.

Just down the trail from Buckskin Joe, Fairplay also was established in 1861. A travel writer noted in 1873 that "the time to see Fairplay is Sunday night. Then it is that all the miners come to town from the hills, and a jolly time they have. The dance and bawdy houses are then in their

element, and money and wine (sometimes blood) flows freely." Some of
the dance houses and variety theaters were next door to the Methodist
church, the only house of worship in town.[4] Over time, smaller camps
around Fairplay would also feature bedroom entertainment; just four
miles away, the mining community of Leavick offered a single bordello
on the edge of town.

North of Fairplay was Breckenridge, notable by 1880 for its numerous saloons and three "honky tonks." Two of these were located in "a
narrow passage" between French Street and Lincoln Avenue.[5] Later
the red-light district, with bordellos called the Blue Goose, Columbine
Rest, and the Pines, developed across the Blue River west of town. One
resident recalled a day when the ladies of Breckenridge's red-light resort
"invaded the town" wearing "flowing costumes, Merry Widow hats and
feather [boas]." The women "hired a fancy rig from the livery stable and
went for a wild ride up and down the streets. They stopped at saloons
for fresh inspiration and descended upon the stores whence respectable
shoppers fled. They were finally routed and returned to their domain by
the sheriff and some hardy aides."[6]

Breckenridge's best-known madam was Minnie Cowell, whose
bordello was on the road to the Wellington Mine. In 1907 Minnie was
robbed at gunpoint by a masked man. Her house had closed for the
night, but two customers upstairs were staying over. From her downstairs room, Minnie was awakened by the sound of a breaking window.
The robber knew where she kept her money, commanding, "Up with
your hands—dig up that trunk key or I'll blow the top of your head off!"
The thief absconded with $340. Minnie told police she recognized the
man's voice as a customer who had been there earlier that night.[7] Minnie
had a soft side; once, after a family with several children lost their home
to fire, the madam bought a new house for them. She remained in Breckenridge as late as 1920, when she employed only one other prostitute.

The general public believed that good time girls had lots of fun. Sometimes, they were right.
Courtesy Jan MacKell Collins.

Those women daring to access Leadville via Mosquito Pass could also access precarious Independence Pass to Aspen, founded in 1879. In Aspen's case, early ordinances included an 1884 five-dollar "tax" on soiled doves. The girls could afford it; when prostitute Fanny Chambers died that year, newspapers took note of her fancy funeral and expensive coffin. By 1885 fifteen bordellos spanned a two-block area of Durant Avenue.

Aspen remained fairly tolerant of the red-light district—at least until the Colorado Midland Railroad built its depot on Deane Street, one block south of Durant Avenue. Disembarking passengers had no choice but to pass through "the jungles of Durant Street" to access the town.[8] The prostitutes of Aspen were politely asked to move to a different locale, which they willingly did—or almost. An 1888 article told of twenty-four bad girls who were brought before the grand jury to discuss the matter. "The nymphs put on their best clothes and endeavored to make as much capital as they could out of the event, parading into the courtroom four abreast, swishing their skirts and tossing their heads in the most approved fashion," commented the *Aspen Evening Chronicle*.[9]

A smaller camp near Leadville was the short-lived shanty settlement of Douglass City. The community was primarily home to workers extending the Colorado Midland Railroad over Hagerman Pass in 1887. The majority of them were Italians, and soon Douglass City hosted eight saloons and a dance hall, all clustered together on one main street. There were no schools, churches, police, or firemen. Those soiled doves who were too jaded to work in Leadville made their way to Douglass City, where shootouts and knife fights were common. According to author Marshall Sprague, the community met its end when the tunnel's dynamite powder house blew up by accident.

The bawdy women at Aspen, Buckskin Joe, Fairplay, and Douglass City were fairly representative of other camp women of Colorado. Far removed from actual cities where laws and lawmen were more frequent, the ladies of the camps experienced more freedom. At the town of Gothic, north of Gunnison, the employees of the town's two dance halls dared to wear their skirts up to their knees—a big no-no in the Victorian era. Also north of Gunnison was Crested Butte, founded in 1879. Almost immediately a series of saloons could be accessed along Elk Avenue and Second Street. Nearby, the Forest Queen Brothel was openly run by a well-known prostitute called "One Eye" Ruby.

Forty miles from Gunnison was Tin Cup, which between 1880 and 1890 featured a booming little red-light district on the south end of Grand Avenue. Old-timers recalled that the girls did not come outside much during the day except to get the occasional bucket of water from a nearby ditch. As Tin Cup's mining era played out, a smaller population of prostitutes moved to an alley behind Washington Avenue. As a child, Eleanor Perry and her friend encountered Tin Can Laura, one of the working girls who happened to be collecting her lacy laundry from a Mrs. Bley. "To Elsie and me, Laura said, 'Be sure and mind your mothers. Your mothers know best. Mind everything your mothers tell you.'" Tin Can Laura later married and left town, but the children remembered her speech and later said it did more for them than any lecture from their own mothers.[10]

At Silver Cliff in the southern portion of the state, the saloon men and shady ladies enjoyed hosting frequent parades and employing a brass band to lead spectators to their businesses. By 1880 the women of the town made no secret of their professions, and the census taker documented them outright as "sporting women." At Arbourville, located along Monarch Pass, the community's social activities were said to have set centered around the only brothel in town. The structure also functioned as a stagecoach stop, saloon, and hotel.

Down the road from Arbourville was Maysville, established in 1879 as the last stop before the Monarch Pass Toll Road into the westernmost Colorado goldfields. Alternately called Crazy Camp and Marysville,

Maysville featured the Eureka Dance Hall and the Palace of Pleasure. When nearby Garfield suffered a fire in 1883, only the town hall and the red-light district survived. In 1880 at the community of Shavano, some ten miles from Maysville, the population of 110 included two women: one respectable wife and one prostitute.

Camps to the south included Creede, founded in about 1889. The settlement was soon jokingly referred to as "Gin Town" for the large quantities of alcohol served there.[11] "I can hear the sound of saws and hammers, the tinkle of pianos, the scrape of violins, the scurry of flying feet in dance-halls, the clink of silver on gambling tables, the sharp bark of six-shooters as some life was snuffed out in the smoke and the maudlin laughter of a dance hall girl as she swung in the arms of some human form," wrote a reporter for the *Saguache Crescent*.[12]

The best known of Creede's infamous deaths was that of Bob Ford, the killer of outlaw Jesse James, who was shot to death in June of 1892. Ford had actually been in Colorado since at least 1889, when he dealt faro for madam Laura Bell McDaniel and other places in Colorado City near Colorado Springs. He was arrested for gambling in December of 1891 and turned away by Sheriff Hi Wilson when he tried to infiltrate Cripple Creek around that same time. Ironically, a story in the *Colorado City Iris* mistakenly reported that Ford had been killed in Creede shortly after he departed Colorado City. Ford was still very much alive, but in June of 1892, Edward O'Kelley indeed shot him to death in his own saloon.

Ford's large funeral procession a few days later was attended by *Creede Daily Chronicle* reporter Hugh Thomason. But Thomason's attention to the matter was diverted by the death of a gentle harlot known as Creede Lily, who was found dead in her tent within a few days of Ford's killing. Most of the throng going to Ford's gravesite overlooked that Creede Lily was being buried that day too, and it was Thomason who spoke over her grave. "Dear God, we are sending you the soul of

Creede Lily," he said. "Thou knowest the burdens she had to bear. Be merciful."[13] Just up the road from Creede was Spar City, with a two-story saloon and dance hall, and the community of Bachelor, with two saloons and a parlor house.

When the mining camp of Bonanza was established in 1880, there wasn't a wayward woman to be found, at first. In a letter to his wife back East, physician Charles Brown commented, "Thus far I have seen no prostitutes in Bonanza, but I understand there will be some soon as they are looking for them every day. Wish they would not come for they are the curse of the camps. There are so many of them diseased that they set men afire and many young men that come to this country with good health go back perfect wrecks to remain so for life. You may never fear me having anything to do with them for if I were single even, I should avoid them."[14]

In contrast to Brown's view, pioneer Anne Ellis was curious about, even sympathetic toward, the prostitutes who inevitably came to town. "In the early days we took the sporting women as we did the saloon, as a matter of course," she wrote in her autobiography, *The Life of an Ordinary Woman*.[15] Although she was just a child the first time her family moved to Bonanza, Anne seemed to appreciate the company of the town's tainted ladies. On one occasion, the girl dared to visit a brothel herself. "And this is what I remember," she later recalled, "first, a strong sweet smell, several pretty girls with lots of lace on their clothes ... one is sitting on the floor in a mess of pillows, two men, dressed and seemingly in their right minds, are sitting there laughing. They give me candy, and I leave after having a very pleasant time." Anne also recalled spending her evenings reading the popular children's book series *Peck's Bad Boy* in the company of a local prostitute named Lil.[16]

Anne's family moved away for a time, but when they returned, the red-light ladies were still there. One of them, a woman named Helen, was working for madam Laura Evens in Salida, some forty miles away.

Laura, "when time and occasions demanded, would send over extra girls," according to Anne, who had grown into a young lady and now worked at the telephone company. When at work, she often overheard Helen's conversations with Laura. "No, don't send Queenie, they don't like her," she heard Helen say once. "Send Grace and Lillie—no, I think they will be enough; there are only about twenty-five men." Helen later married a saloonkeeper and went "respectable," but Bonanza's elite social circles disapproved of her. Once, when she was invited to bring a donation to the community Christmas tree, Anne heard one woman, Mrs. Smeltzer, say, "If old Helen comes, I will climb her frame." Helen was sent a bag of candy instead. In time she grew weary of being ostracized, began drinking heavily and fighting, and eventually "went back to her old life."[17]

One of Colorado's most colorful madams during the early 1900s was Ada Smith, who called herself Dixie, of Montezuma. Although the small town had strict ordinances prohibiting prostitution, Dixie determinedly maintained her tidy white cottage of pleasure just off Main Street for many years. Sometimes she worked alone; sometimes she employed up to two or three girls. At all times, she adored wearing "gaudy colors, gauzy scarves, and big picture hats, and worked hard to ingrain herself within the community. She shopped locally at the mercantile owned by the Rice family and conducted herself so professionally that the whole family eventually felt comfortable waiting on her."[18]

Dixie also supported Montezuma's baseball team, adhering to the rule that she sit at the end of the stands and away from the decent folks. Still, she dressed in her very best for each game, "catching stares as she hollered for the home team." Dixie also shopped smart, collecting coupons by saving the labels from her canned goods. One of her regular purchases was a case of canned Columbine milk, which she fed to the cats and dogs around town. In addition, she brought food to her clients as they aged, cared for them when they were ill, and joined her girls to care for everyone during the 1918 flu epidemic.[19] It is no wonder that women like Dixie earned the euphemistic nickname of the day, "whore with a heart of gold."

Although there was no gold to be had on Colorado's eastern plains, a few towns along various trails also sported fancy women. At the earlier town of Sedgwick near Bonanza there were two dance halls where "the giddy mazes of the dance can be enjoyed with giddier girls from Silver Cliff and adjoining towns." The cost of a dance was a dollar, fifty cents higher than most other camps. "But the freights you know," said one local paper, "are high in this country."[20]

JANE BOWEN

---•◦•---

The Sage Hen of Silverton

No sooner had it been founded in 1875 than Silverton became notable for its itinerant prostitutes. Although plenty of mines and small camps dotted several areas along the Animas River, none were large enough to support "more than around twelve prostitutes into the early 1880s." Working girls who ventured into the San Juan Mountains above the town found them cold, barren, and harsh. Although it too was subject to debilitating snowstorms in winter, Silverton, located at over 9,300 feet in altitude, offered some of the only real civilization for miles. Blair Street, just off the main drag, proved to be the logical place for a red-light district; the railroad brought in new passengers just a block away. Those respectable people who lived on Blair Street renamed parts of the thoroughfare Empire Street to distinguish themselves from the soiled doves. In time, only the respectable people lived on the west side of town as the gamblers, saloon men, and prostitutes remained on Blair Street in Silverton's "notorious" side of town.

Silverton's first permanent madam was Jane Bowen, who also went by "Sage Hen" as well as the kindly euphemism "Aunt Jane." Born in England, Jane had lived in an area known as "Petticoat Lane" on London's East Side before migrating to America. When and where she met her husband, William, remains unknown. The couple first

Silverton's Blair Street still offers obscure passageways behind the town's former bordellos.
Courtesy Jan MacKell Collins.

appeared together in the 1870 census at Kansas City, Missouri. William toiled as a laborer; Jane kept house. Living with them was a four-year-old named Emma, who had been born in Missouri and was adopted by the Bowens.[1]

Between 1875 and 1878 the Bowens moved to Silverton. Finding the red-light market "quite limited," Jane saw a viable way to make money by hiring prostitutes. She also is credited with opening the first variety show in town. The 1880 census records William Bowen working as a merchant. Jane; her daughter Emma, who was now thirteen years old; and a young lady, twenty-four-year-old Frankie Hanus, also resided in the Bowen home. In the case of Jane and Frankie, their occupations were left blank.[2] The absence of Jane's occupation was not unusual. Both the 1880 and 1885 censuses for Colorado left the majority of prostitutes off-record, even though working girls were likely scattered all through the budding cities and camps of the San

Juan Mountains. One writer speculated that "it is highly probable that, either through personal sensitivities or neglect, the census takers over-looked them in other camps."[3]

Local histories verify that the Bowens purchased a liquor license and opened a saloon and dance hall soon after their arrival. Jane's endeavors earned her the nickname "Pioneer Madam of Blair Street."[4] She ran the operations in Silverton while William ran a ranch with a saloon and boardinghouse some seventeen miles south of town on the Animas Toll Road. It was the perfect place from which miners coming out of the San Juans could be directed to Jane's place at Silverton, which became known as "Westminster Hall." Locals called it "Aunt Jane's Abode for the Fallen."[5]

Early on, the Bowens met with troubles that were, at the time, typical of frontier Colorado. In 1881 William Bowen shot and killed employee John Haley in a dispute over money. Haley and the boss had apparently been arguing about the matter for several days, wherein Bowen accused Haley of stealing from him. One day Haley got drunk and started calling Bowen names. After several fisticuffs, Haley beat Bowen silly and threatened to "kill him before midnight." When Haley returned from his cabin with his hand in his pocket, Bowen was ready with his own revolver. Onlookers warned the weakling Bowen "to look out or he'd be killed." But when Haley advanced on him, Bowen shot him, once. The bullet failed to faze Haley, and Bowen shot twice more, killing him. Bowen went on trial and was found innocent by self-defense.[6]

Jane too was frequently summoned to court, but she and William were well-liked around town. To alleviate being so much in the public eye, the Bowens moved their business out of the glare of the main street to their residence in back of the dance hall in about 1884. They also sent Emma off to school in a faraway place. And despite the reputation of their notorious businesses, the Bowens told the Colorado census taker in 1885 that William was a just a merchant and that Jane was just a housewife. The locals, as well as Silverton's newspaper, the *Silverton Standard*, knew better. A typical ad for Jane's dance hall appeared in the paper on April 5, 1890, proclaiming, "Jane Bowen's hall was opened for the season on Monday evening. Whipple and Shields are providing the music."[7]

William presumably gave up his roadhouse on the Animas Toll Road, perhaps because he was suffering from miner's consumption, a common ailment of those who worked among metallic or mineral dust particles. In late 1890 or early 1891, William took a trip to California in the hope that a change in climate might ease his symptoms. "William Bowen returned home from California on Wednesday," the *Standard* reported in April. "In spite of the long blockade and the reported hard winter here, he found the streets bare and the Westminster Hall running on full time, as it has done all winter. Bill is little under the weather but expects to be alright in a few days."[8] But poor Bill was not alright, succumbing to his illness on June 22, 1891. Jane buried her husband in Silverton's Hillside Cemetery with a modest tombstone and carried on.

In the following months, Jane may have experienced financial hardships. In July of 1891 an advertisement appeared in the *Standard*. "For Sale Cheap," the ad read. "Forty yards of Brussels carpet with nice border. Will be sold cheap. Apply to Mrs. Jane Bowen." Then in March 1892, "Jane Bowen sold her house and lot on Thursday to Joe Sartore, and will leave for England in a few days," according to the *Standard*. The newspaper also decided to send the Sage Hen off with a joke. "Jane is an old landmark in Silverton," the news item ended. "She has resided in Silverton for—but we don't want to tell you how long for fear you might figure out her age." Jane did leave for England. A few weeks later the *Standard* reported that "George Davis is making rapid progress with Jane Bowen's building on Blair Street and will have it all completed by the middle of next month."[9]

Jane did return to Silverton, but her habit of visiting England continued over the next several years. She was likely in back in Silverton in 1893 when her nephew, John Louis, died suddenly at her place. Louis had only been in Silverton for about three weeks on a visit, and unfortunately there was not enough money to return his body to England. He too was buried in Hillside Cemetery. A second nephew visited Jane in 1895, and his visit was nearly as disastrous as that of John Louis. "Last Friday Jane Bowen discovered that someone had put carbolic acid in the food at her house," reported the *Standard*. "As she states, her nephew, Hyman Morris, who has been here about three months, is the guilty party. She had some trouble with him and he tried in this way to get even. He left the first of the week for his home in Brooklyn." What exactly the trouble was remains unknown, but Morris stayed in Brooklyn with his wife, Pauline. As far as anyone knows, he never had contact with Jane again.[10]

Jane rallied from the actions of her naughty nephew, deciding to promote her dance hall with vigor. In October a new advertisement appeared in the *Standard*. "There will be a grand masquerade ball at the Palace Hall on Monday night, November 6," the paper announced. "Great preparations are now being made for the occasion. Masks will be furnished at the hall for all who desire them. Don't forget the place. Palace Hall, Mrs. Jane Bowen, proprietress."[11] In February 1895 a news reporter visited the dance hall. "We suddenly found ourselves on the premises of Jane Bowen," the writer recalled. "It was a strange mixture of erring youth, vigorous manhood and grinning decay." All manner of men were there, from young boys to old men, "all in the mad whirl and excitement of the moment, forgetting the past, present and future." Reigning over all of them was Jane, "bedecked in costly jewels." Jane told the reporter that the prostitution industry was "not very good" and that, alternatively, she preferred to keep her house "more as a house of refuge and rest for the fallen ones of the earth."[12]

Meanwhile, Emma Bowen began appearing in Denver beginning in about 1895, where the Denver City Directory shows her living at 1650 California Street. The address was the location of St. Catherine's Home, "a home for Catholic working girls."[13] Emma, or Emily as she was sometimes known, was still living at St. Catherine's when she committed suicide in February 1898. Although nothing about the incident appears to have been published in Silverton's newspaper, the *Aspen Weekly Times* of February 17 verified that Emma had killed herself by swallowing "Rough on Rats," an extremely poisonous rodent killer containing arsenic mixed with coal. "She was in ill health and despondent because unable to work," the paper explained. "She died at 6 o'clock this morning. Bowen was the adopted daughter of a woman of the same name in Silverton, Colorado and she frequently received money and clothing from her adopted mother. She was about 28 years of age."[14] Emily was buried under the name "Emlie" Bowen at Mount Olivet Cemetery in today's Wheat Ridge.

In the wake of the tragedy, Jane fled to England again. Virtually nothing is known of her family there or what she did while in the UK, but it can be safely guessed that she found comfort in visiting her old family home and friends. Jane appears to have kept a watchful eye on her property in Silverton, returning briefly in December 1899 before departing for England once more. This time two years passed before the *Standard* reported in February 1902, "A letter came to Silverton announcing that Jane Bowen, familiarly known in the halcyon days of Silverton as 'Sage Hen,' will soon return from England and will start up the Palace dance hall on the corner of 12th and Blair." This time, Jane had been gone so long that it took some time to revive the dance hall. "Once again will the Palace dance hall echo with the strains of music, the tread of dancing feet and the clink of the inspiring schooner," warned the *Standard* in March. "Once again will a familiar voice admonish the throng not to 'lift the roof off me 'ouse.' For the Sage Hen, nee Mrs. Jane Bowen, has returned from London after an absence of about two years to conduct this frivolous resort." A week after the article appeared, a second notice in the paper announced that Jane had purchased a liquor license from fellow saloon owner Albert Swanson.[15]

Once more, Jane's place opened to an excited public. "Aunt Jane says, boys from the 'ills hare hinvited to fall 'round hand take ha glass hat 'er hexpense!" according to one source.[16] The Palace Hall was indeed once again alive and well and popular. On at least one occasion, in 1904, Jane was taken to court for disturbing the peace and fined $21.50. Did Jane tell anyone that she was making one last romp through Silverton to earn money for her retirement? Probably not. The news was likely quite a surprise when the *Silverton Standard* published the last news about Jane Bowen in its July 8, 1905, issue: "The 'Aunt Jane' or 'Sage Hen' but known properly as the Jane Bowen Dance Hall was this week sold to Peter Orella, consideration $3,500."[17] Jane left Silverton a final time, presumably for her beloved England, and was heard from no more.

MATTIE SILKS

Denver's Enduring Madam

For over fifty years after its founding, Colorado's "Queen City," Denver, enjoyed generations of illicit fun. Within two years of the 1858 arrival of Denver's first Anglo prostitute, Ada LaMont, bordellos were springing up like wildflowers. By 1860 entrepreneur Charley Harrison was Ada's paramour, running the Criterion saloon as well as two bordellos. A female visitor to Denver in 1868 was mortified at the number of prostitutes running amok in the city. "Such a collection of fiends in human shape I hope never to see again," she declared in a letter home. "I did not meet more than two of my own sex who made the most distant claims to even common decency or self-respect."[1] The authorities felt the same way, and in 1870 ordinances were passed in the city of Denver prohibiting prostitution.

Rather than go away, Denver's brothel owners simply formed a neighborhood of their own. By the time the railroad premiered in Denver in the late 1860s, the city's demimonde spanned four blocks in an area around Larimer and McGaa Streets. Hop Alley, between Larimer and McGaa, was home to some eight hundred Chinese that included about fifty "slave girls" at any given time. In time, Denver's red-light district featured over a thousand working girls. Their workplaces included "cribs"—small, two-room apartments for lower-rent, unrefined ladies—and fancy parlor houses where only cultured and educated women could find work. McGaa Street was later renamed Holladay Street after Ben Holladay, as revenge after the livery owner closed down a favored stage line.[2]

Denver's most famous madam arrived in 1876. Her name was Mattie Silks, and for the next fifty-four years, she was a force to be reckoned with. Mattie was born Martha A. Nimon in Fayette County, Pennsylvania, in 1845. Her parents, Henry and Sarah, toiled as farmers while raising their five children. By 1850 the family had migrated to Erie, Indiana. Mattie remained with her family through at least 1860, but had traveled to Kansas, or perhaps Springfield, Illinois, by 1865. There, according to various historians, she may have worked as a freighter on wagon trains traveling between St. Joseph, Missouri, and Colorado, or perhaps followed her chosen profession, prostitution. Most historians do agree that a sign on one of her first parlor houses read "Men taken in and done for" and that she was run out of Olathe, Kansas, before working the cattle trails out of Kansas City during the summer months. Mattie always maintained that she never worked as a prostitute herself, but simply oversaw the employees of her businesses.[3]

Mattie eventually drove a wagon with four girls—three from Abilene and one from Dodge City—to the Pikes Peak region, making her way from mining camp to mining camp. Her wagon contained a "portable boarding house for young ladies," really just a canvas tent which did include a canvas bathtub.[4] The wagon eventually made its way to Denver, where the ladies visited the "Elephant Corral" and "behaved with the 'utmost decorum'" before traveling west to the mining camp of Jamestown. At such places, Mattie wisely knew to set up her own camp below town, "because prospective patrons would more willingly walk down a mountainside than climb it."[5]

By 1875 Mattie was in Georgetown, where she operated her first real brothel. Her girls were touted as the "fairest frails in town." Mattie herself claimed she was very particular about her girls. "I never took a girl into my house who had had no previous experience of life and men," she said. "That was a rule of mine . . . No innocent, young girl was ever hired by me. Those with experience came to me for the same reasons that I hired them. Because there was money in it for all of us." Also in Georgetown, Mattie met, and perhaps married, Casey (or George) Silks, a faro dealer from Pueblo who had dealt cards at several mining camps around Colorado. Mattie may have met Silks as early as 1866. If she didn't marry him, she certainly lived as his common-law wife for at least a few years.[6]

Much has been written about whether Mattie ever had children, for they were certainly a presence in her life. One of them, Benjamin, is thought by some historians to have come of the union between Mattie and Casey Silks. But neither her husband nor the child appear with Mattie on Clear Creek property tax rolls for 1875 or a tax assessment list in 1876, where Mattie is recorded as residing in Georgetown and working as a "manufactured liquor dealer."[7]

While Mattie was in Indiana for a visit in June of 1880, the census taker noted that she was either widowed or divorced. Below Mattie's name was that of seven-year-old Benjamin Silks, who was born in Indiana. But Benjamin is also listed as a "nephew" to Mattie's father. It should also be noted that Mattie's sister, Henrietta, gave birth to her son, Nimon Benjamin Keller, in Indiana in about 1872, making him of the same age and same birthplace as Benjamin Silks. The boy does not appear in subsequent census records or any written documentation regarding Mattie or Casey Silks. Who he really was unfortunately lies in the hands of the census taker, who, in recording the boy's information directly following Mattie's, could easily have written incorrect information about him. Mattie's mother died the following month, which could have been the reason for her visit.

What is known for sure about Mattie is that she eventually split with Silks, by death or divorce. But she kept his name (it was, after all, quite alluring for a woman in her profession) and next took up with Cortez D.

Thomson. Born in Alabama around 1850, Thomson's large family had moved to Kansas City, Missouri, by 1870. His father was a respectable bookkeeper. Nineteen-year-old Thomson was a clerk for the railroad, a job he held through at least 1871, when he took off for parts unknown. In Georgetown he met Mattie, and the two moved to Denver together in 1877. Thus began a tempestuous relationship as Mattie and Cort fought and clawed their way along with each other over the next two decades.

Mattie had no sooner arrived in Denver than the March 28, 1877, issue of the *Rocky Mountain News* reported that "Madame Silks was fined $12 for drunkenness, and paid it like a little woman. She ought to play it finer when she gets on a spree."[8] Mattie did "play it finer," first renting and then purchasing the first of her many brothels, at 501 Holladay Street. The house was large and could accommodate up to twelve employees. She was in business by June, when she was again hauled into court with some other women "under the ordinance for the registration of lewd women" and paid fifteen dollars.[9] Then, in August, an infamous incident involving a supposed duel between Mattie and fellow madam Katie Fulton over Cort Thomson occurred.

Historians have had a high time expounding on the "duel." One source says Katie showed up at an engagement party hosted by Mattie and Thomson at the Olympic Gardens and accused Mattie of "stealing her man."[10] Others have followed author Max Miller's ridiculous claim that Mattie and Katie actually stripped to their waists before duking it out. Still others say the women took their shots but missed—save for Katie's stray bullet, which struck Thomson in the neck.

The best source comes from the only documentation of the time, the *Denver Daily Times*, which reported that Katie and Mattie had an argument following a footrace. Thomson won the race, and Mattie collected $2,000. A fight broke out involving several people, including Mattie, Thomson, Katie, and Katie's friend Sam Thatcher. Katie received the worst of it: During the fray she was punched, knocked down twice, and kicked in the face, breaking her nose. Afterward, as Thomson returned to Denver in a buggy, another carriage pulled up beside him and he was shot in the neck, though not fatally. Katie left town for a while but returned to Denver in September, where she had another fight with Mattie. This time, Mattie punched Katie, knocking her down and injuring her nose again.

Most historians agree that Cort and Mattie were engaged around the time the "duel" occurred. Cort was an exciting man: He was good-looking, a gambler, and a champion sprinter for various fire departments who won lots of races and lots of bets. Historically speaking, there are numerous rumors, some true, regarding Cort and his past. He may have had a wife and daughter, either in Georgetown or back in Texas, and claimed to have served in the Civil War. Alternatively, the wife and daughter resided somewhere in the East, and Thomson's wife decreed there would be no divorce unless she died.

Mattie's love for Thomson was deep. She was willing to put up with his drinking and gambling habits, both of which he often financed with her money. Mattie once commented that she wished he would learn how to play cards more "effectively" but that she "guessed he never would."[11] On those rare occasions when he won at the tables, Thomson would buy small gifts for Mattie. She didn't mind that the gifts were from money she had given him, and despite two terrible beatings Thomson gave her, she apparently loved him too much to leave him.

Mattie weathered Thomson's antics while tending to business. In 1878 she purchased a second brothel from Nellie French on Holladay Street for $13,000. Her holdings now included houses at 500, 501, and 502 Holladay Street. Mattie remained at 501 and rented out the other buildings to other madams. In 1879 she purchased two lots in town. When madam Jennie Rogers arrived in Denver that year, Mattie sold her one of the brothels and wisely formed an alliance with her. Once, after the city of Denver decreed that all fallen women must identify themselves by wearing a yellow ribbon on their arms, Mattie and Jennie had their employees dress in yellow from head to toe and parade all over town. The authorities quickly repealed the order. Despite their friendship, however, the two must have had at least some competitive feelings toward each other. Jennie called herself the "Queen of the Colorado Underworld," which surely irked Mattie.[12]

Mattie's personal and business life continued in its erratic fashion over the next several years. In 1880 she purchased more property, made the trip to Indiana to see her family, and forked over $250 when Cort Thomson lost a race in Greeley. The following year, the first tragedy on record occurred at Mattie's when one of her girls, Mattie Woods, committed suicide by taking chloroform. Then in August, Cort was suspected of participating in a rigged race and was arrested. Mattie, of course, bailed him out of jail. In between these incidents, Mattie battled with the authorities over new ordinances. In 1882, after witnessing soiled doves participating in horse races, water fights to show off their physical attributes, and public pillow fights, the city outlawed soliciting and required curtains on all brothel windows. Lower-class houses ripped "accidental" holes in the curtains, allowing passersby their own private peep show. Mattie's parlor houses, which were more refined, likely refrained from the practice.

In 1883 Cort Thomson was living at an address on Larimer Street in downtown Denver. The next year he and Mattie married, supposedly after Thomson learned his wife had died. The two were united in matrimony in Miami County, Indiana, on July 6, 1884, and Mattie purchased yet another bordello in 1884. In the 1885 Denver directory, Cort still lived on Larimer, working as a stock dealer. It is not known if Mattie lived there too, but later that same year her parlor house was the scene of a scam. A man, who had taken part in the theft of several hundred-dollar printing plates back East two years earlier, showed up in Denver with counterfeit bills. One surfaced at Mattie's parlor house after the girl on duty sold the man a five-dollar bottle of wine. He paid with the fake bill, leaving immediately after receiving his ninety-five dollars in change.

Beginning in 1886, more mysterious children surfaced in Mattie's life. Several historians say that Cort Thomson's daughter died during childbirth and that Mattie convinced him to adopt his granddaughter.[13] She also purchased a ranch on the eastern plains at Wray around this time, possibly as a suitable place to raise the girl and also as a means to keep Thomson out of trouble. Mattie loved horses and raised "racing steeds" at the ranch, which were entered into races at Overland Park in Denver.[14] The mystery of the child deepened further in September of 1887, when the *Rocky Mountain News* reported that "Nettie Silks, an adopted daughter of the notorious Mattie Silks, was taken from Mrs. Seymour's house of ill fame by the officers yesterday and sent by Judge Campbell to the House of the Good Shepherd until April 22, when she will have attained majority."[15] Nettie's exact identity remains unknown.

Mattie Silks (left) at her Wray ranch with one of her beautiful steeds. The girl beside her might be the mysterious Theresa Thomson, who was born in 1890.
Courtesy Denver Public Library.

What is known for sure is that Mattie purchased yet another bordello at 1916 Market Street, formerly Holladay Street, in 1887. Although she continued buying and selling other properties over time, Mattie would keep the house at 1916 Market for several years. The classy and elegantly styled building towered two stories and featured a wrought-iron widow's walk on top, awnings over the windows, stone steps, and a quaint flower box out front. Clearly, this building shone in comparison with lesser parlor houses in Denver, and the authorities recognized it as such. When police raided the girls from the low-rent "cribs" of Holladay Street in May of 1889, parlor houses like Mattie's remained unmolested.

The year 1890 began with Mattie finding herself in Aspen, where for the first time since 1877, she was again fined for being drunk in public. The date of her infraction was January 21.[16] Five days later, according to certain historians and even her descendants, Mattie gave birth to a child, Theresa Louise Thomson. But Theresa later identified her father as "C. D. Thomson" and her mother as "Jeanette Miller."[17] If Thomson was the father of the child and Mattie was not the mother, the madam deserves much credit for taking the child in. Very little else is known about Theresa. Over time, she would be identified as a "niece" to Mattie. Whoever she was, Theresa maintained some sort of maternal relationship with Mattie and was part of her life for many more years.

Meanwhile, Cort Thomson just couldn't seem to stay out of trouble. If Mattie thought the horse ranch at Wray might keep him occupied, she was wrong. In about October 1890, Thomson and a handful of other men were discovered to have stolen "several car loads of cattle" which were shipped to Kansas City. When the police closed in on the scheme, Thomson fled to Texas, where he was apprehended and returned to a Colorado jail. Around this time Mattie, probably sick of her husband's antics and perhaps his infidelity, took up for a short time with a wealthy railroad executive who asked her to accompany him to California. The trip included a side jaunt to the Wyoming ranch of the exceedingly wealthy entrepreneur Potter Palmer, where Mattie was introduced as her companion's wife.[18]

Thomson's thoughts on Mattie's excursion remain unrecorded, but the relationship came to a head in 1891, when Mattie caught her husband with prostitute Lillie Dab of Leadville. Mattie fired a shot at the harlot, clipping two curls off of Lillie's coiffured head. Lillie scrambled out of the room while Thomson wrestled the pistol from Mattie, clubbed her on the head, and gave her an "unmerciful beating."[19] In March Mattie sued for divorce, claiming that Thomson "knocked her down, blackened her eye, beat her face and body and kicked her while she was lying on the floor in a most cruel and brutal way." She also let the court know that she had paid for three parcels of land in Yuma County that were in Thomson's name and accused him of squandering "between forty-five thousand and fifty thousand dollars" of her money. Thomson offered to put the land in Mattie's name and softened her up enough that she dropped the divorce.[20]

A year later, March of 1892, soiled doves Effie Pryor and Allie Ellis decided to commit mutual suicide at Mattie's 1916 Market Street parlor house. The girls made their decision following a night of heavy drinking, in response to Allie's boyfriend leaving her. Approaching a pharmacy clerk, the girls had made a trade: The young man could take "pornographic" pictures of them in exchange for some morphine. The girls were found "lying on their backs, side by side, disrobed and gasping for breath, their faces black and distorted." A doctor was summoned and Effie was saved, but Allie died a few days later.[21] Suicides were just one of any number of hazards in the prostitution industry. This and other incidents hardly prevented Mattie from expanding her business and acquiring the bordello next door to her in about 1893.

In July of 1895, Denver detectives received a tip that a young boy living at Mattie's brothel was actually an eleven-year-old girl. The officers discovered the child, as well as five-year-old Theresa Thomson.

Although the officers removed the other child, they apparently did not take Theresa, who they may have believed was Mattie's daughter and who was being cared for despite living in a whorehouse. The "boy" was taken to police headquarters and insisted her name was Willie Evans. When officers pressed the issue, she broke down and revealed she was Jennie Johns and that she had been the victim of abuse at the hands of her stepfather, Thomas Sutton. Newspapers reported Jennie had been taken from Rock Springs, Wyoming, by her father, William Johns, in order to keep her from having to testify at a preliminary hearing against Sutton. A prominent Rock Springs businessman, Sutton had been accused of an attempted rape on Jennie and had already assaulted the girl's thirteen-year-old sister. Mrs. Sutton, working with Johns, had dressed Jennie in boy's clothing and brought her to Denver. As the story unfolded further, Sutton claimed he had paid Johns to "kidnap" the girl to escape prosecution. Johns denied this, saying he only wanted to keep her from having to testify regarding a "sex matter." Sutton fled, and Jennie was reunited with her mother.[22]

In 1897, during one of their honeymoon phases, Cort and Mattie Thomson took excursions to Great Britain and Alaska. In the latter, Mattie opened a brothel in Dawson City, Canada, but found it too cold. She did net $38,000 after only three months and returned to Colorado. She also remained by Cort's side when his mother became gravely ill at the Wray ranch in 1899. By 1900, the honeymoon was over. In March, Thomson went on another drinking spree in Denver in celebration of his birthday. With him was one Kid Burns, and the two tore it up at Pennington's Saloon before announcing they were going to the ranch, selling off the cattle, and heading for the Klondike.

A furious Mattie secured a warrant for her husband's arrest, but Thomson escaped prosecution by getting the sheriff drunk. Soon after returning to Wray with Burns, Thomson "celebrated their arrival by riding up and down the sidewalks and announcing that if he had his

45-caliber revolver he would clean up the town." Instead of heading for the Klondike, Thomson fell horribly ill from drinking and taking opium, as well as a possible batch of bad oysters. As always, Mattie hastened to his side. She arrived at the Commercial Hotel in Wray with Theresa on April 10. Thomson was slumped in a rocking chair and allegedly accused Mattie of hiring someone to poison him. "If I had a gun, I would kill you," he is supposed to have said. If the story is true, Mattie placed her pistol in his hand and responded, "If you're going to die, I don't want to live."[23]

The only certainty of this tale is that Thomson did die, without firing a shot. Mattie had his body returned to Denver, where he was buried in Fairmount Cemetery. In reporting Thomson's death, the *Fort Morgan Times* identified Mattie as being "known in the half world of Denver" but commented that "her grief seemed to be deep and genuine." And, there may be some truth to Thomson's dying threat. "One wonders how a woman's love can cling to such a creature," the paper commented. "In his drunken frenzy he had beaten and abused her up to within a few hours of his death."[24]

In June when the census was taken, Mattie was at her ranch. With her was ten-year-old Theresa, identified as Mattie's niece. Theresa could read and write, according to the document. She also had attended school. The 1900 census also asked women whether they had any children, living or dead. Mattie replied no to both.

In 1905 Mattie found at least some redemption for Cort Thomson's mistreatment of her. She took up with John Dillon Ready, aka "Handsome Jack," a longtime friend who became Mattie's "bookkeeper, bouncer and general helper." Mattie's cook and housekeeper, Janie Green, remembered him as "very good looking but bossy toward Mattie," whom he said he had to take care of "because she [was] getting old."[25] It was true, for Ready was eighteen years younger than sixty-year-old Mattie. The 1905 Denver directory shows him living at 1916

Market Street, and in 1906 he signed as a witness to Mattie's filing an official homestead claim on her ranch. The two visited there often. By 1911 the couple had moved to Mattie's fashionable quarters at 2635 Lawrence Street, away from the red-light district. Mattie did, however, continue overseeing her many brothels on Market Street.

In 1908, after years of authorities mostly looking the other way with regard to the red-light district, District Attorney George Stidger became determined to overthrow police and shut down the houses of ill fame. Using an upcoming election as his tool, Stidger claimed the red-light district "rolls up ten thousand illegal votes for the police machine every election through the agency of its padded rooming houses and willing repeaters." He then gave notice to Denver's prostitutes that they had twenty-four hours to secure decent employment or leave town.[26]

If Stidger's threats disturbed Mattie, she hardly showed it, as she and John Ready nestled in their Lawrence Street home while other madams ran Mattie's houses. Not surprisingly, one of them was none other than Theresa Thomson, who in 1910 was running the 1916 Market Street house. Theresa employed a cook and several young women between the ages of twenty-one and thirty-three.

In January 1911 Mattie purchased the infamous House of Mirrors at 1942 Market Street from the estate of Jennie Rogers. For a time, she lived at the new parlor house and appears to have run it herself. Janie Green was working for her by 1912 and verified that Mattie's employees at the House of Mirrors split their earnings with the madam. They were expected to pay room and board out of their half, plus pay back Mattie for any clothing they charged to her account with local merchants. The rent did include two nutritious meals each day, breakfast at 11:30 a.m. and dinner at 5:00 p.m., before the house opened for business. Green also said Mattie had a few fancy call girls residing in Denver's upscale hotels who could make house calls as needed.

Janie did not mention that 1912 was the year that Denver police commissioner George Creel, like George Stidger, began making a concerted effort to clean up Market Street. Creel was more successful, enlisting the assistance of social worker Josephine Roche to downsize the number of prostitutes in town from 700 to just 250. Creel's methodology was something to be admired: The lawman saw prostitutes as victims and felt the best way to reform them was to remove them from the red-light district, treat them for any venereal diseases they had contracted, and teach them "new trades and skills." Any women arrested for prostitution would be able to work off their time at Denver's rural County Farm. There, they could be treated for illnesses or addictions as they learned a better way of life.

Although Creel and Roche were able to downsize the red-light district in just six months, the presumption that prostitutes were working against their will was largely misguided. When Creel was unable to procure the poor farm for his use, he used the House of the Good Shepherd in Denver instead. The place was too close to the downtown area, however. To his disappointment, Creel found that at least some of the women went back to the profession, where they could make money faster than they would have at the menial jobs they were taught.[27]

Madams like Mattie Silks paid little attention to Creel's efforts, likely because her girls were healthier and wiser than the average soiled dove. The House of Mirrors exuded the grandeur of a wealthy home. Musician George Morrison remembered his engagements at Mattie's for a couple of years beginning in 1913. When the band played at parlor houses, he said, "they wanted mostly kind of quiet music. And they didn't want any long pieces. Short, very short maybe two choruses." The madams, he said, "never allowed the girls to dance, you know. The music was there for music lovers that wanted to hear some nice numbers and maybe once in a while a dance number."[28]

But there was, as usual, a darker side to the House of Mirrors. On New Year's night in 1913, police were summoned. They were accompanied by reporter Forbes Parkhill, who said Mattie was now "short, quite fat, and wore spectacles." Mattie, looking grim, led them to the room of "Stella," who wore nothing but a pair of "black openwork stockings" and writhed in agony from swallowing poison as the piano played gaily downstairs. As the men carried her downstairs, she threw up on Parkhill. She was taken to the hospital but died the next day. How many times had Mattie witnessed such a scene in her own house, and how much longer could she take being a red-light madam?[29]

The authorities began shutting down Market Street in 1915, a process that took some time; twenty-nine prostitutes were arrested the following year. The year after that, eighty-two women were charged with prostitution. Finally, in 1918, Mattie sold the House of Mirrors to the Buddhist Temple. She did keep the house at 1922 Market Street, where John Ready still worked as a janitor. By 1920 Mattie appears to have retired, turning 1916 Market Street into the Silks Hotel. Theresa Thomson was in Denver too, now working as a laundress and boarding at the home of her cousin, Henrietta Thomas. Mattie finally married John Ready on May 1, 1923. Theresa had moved to Washington by then, where she too married in 1924. Her life as a housewife remained uneventful and she died in 1967, with nobody the wiser to her past.

In 1928 historians began poking around, exploring the history of Denver's demimonde. One of them, a reporter for the *Rocky Mountain News*, managed to interview Mattie. By then, the elderly madam was confined to a wheelchair after breaking her hip two years earlier. To the young reporter, she was "a frail, tiny old woman with transparent skin, faded watery eyes, a kindly expression." Later that year, on Christmas Day, Mattie got out of her wheelchair and fell, breaking her hip a final time.[30]

Mattie Silks died on January 7, 1929, at the age of eighty-three. Her final estate wasn't much, but she had already given a lot of her jewelry to Theresa. Her money and property were divided equally between Theresa and John Ready, including the ranch at Wray. Mattie is buried in Denver's Fairmount Cemetery under the name Martha A. Ready, allegedly near the unmarked grave of Cort Thomson. John Ready died in Wray in 1931 and was buried near Mattie.

Mattie's tumultuous life as a leading madam in Denver was best summed up by the lady herself. "Said the man didn't live who had money enough to buy her, and claimed she never had anything to do with any man, except if she loved him," Janie Green said. "Sometimes she would cry a little and say she was sorry she was a sporting lady, and if she had her life to live over she would go into some other line, because running a sporting house was a very uncertain line of business, what with the law and all."[31]

JENNIE ROGERS

---•◦•---

Queen of the Colorado Underworld

Mattie Silks's biggest competitor was Jennie Rogers, aka Leah J. Tehme. Very little is known about her early life, except for her birth on July 4, 1843, in Allegheny, Pennsylvania. She had a half-sister, Annie, who was born in 1845, and her father, James Weaver, was in the produce business. Jennie spent at least some of her time growing up selling the family produce on the streets. In about 1860 she married Dr. James C. Fries, sometimes identified as G. Friess.

The union proved too dull for Jennie, and she allegedly ran away with a steamboat captain named Rogers. The man named his ship the *Jennie Rogers* and traveled with Jennie throughout Pennsylvania and Ohio. After a few years Jennie tired of life on the river, eventually taking a job as a housekeeper for the mayor of Pittsburgh. In time, stories of her leaving her husband and her previous affairs surfaced and the mayor was forced to fire her to save his image. He did, however, pay her a substantial amount of "hush" money—enough to start a "fashionable resort" in the demimonde of St. Louis.[1]

After a few years, Jennie decided to follow the gold rush to Colorado. On January 15, 1880, she bought her first brothel at 527 Holladay Street from madam Mattie Silks. The price was $4,600. It was said the St. Louis chief of police, Jennie's personal friend, would come to visit, and that Jennie even had a portrait of him hanging in her brothel. Her admirers were many, and for good reason: Jennie has been described as a tall, raven-haired beauty who favored wearing velvet dresses and emerald earrings. She was known to be "hot-tempered" yet "well-spoken" and "not given to profanities." Even so, Jennie suffered her first arrest in March, along with madam Eva Lewis, for "unladylike conduct in the streets." The ladies, it seemed, put on too much of a show while riding their horses through town.[2]

Jennie got her act together and quickly. On June 18, 1880, she officially obtained a divorce from James C. Fries. When her horse slipped on the ice the following winter and pitched her onto Holladay Street, the newspaper merely identified her as being "well-known in this city." Jennie continued purchasing properties on Market Street and other places around Denver. By 1886 she owned an astounding six parlor houses, including one next door to her first one, onto which she constructed a connecting corridor.[3]

Jennie paid her fines regularly and weathered several arrests. During an 1886 raid, she and fourteen other madams were fined seventy-five dollars. In court, it was revealed that District Attorney LeDru Rhodes had paid twenty-five dollars to two men, one of them a police officer, to gain entry to Jennie's parlor house and "lay traps for their victims" so they could take the madam to court. Those in the courtroom regarded the entrapment as "little less than blackmail" and further voiced their opinions that the women should be acquitted. Jennie was fined anyway.[4]

By 1887 Jennie had another new address, 1950 Holladay Street, which officials had renamed Market Street. She had the building constructed herself, and until she died, the parlor house remained one of her fanciest. David Mechling, whose drugstore was located between Jennie's parlor house and the meeting rooms of the Colorado legislature, noted that each afternoon around three o'clock, after their meetings, the local senators and representatives would make their way down to Jennie's. In 1889 the madam built her most famous brothel of all, the House of Mirrors, at 1942 Market Street. The architect was William Quayle, who also designed the First Congregational Church and later West High School.

Although Jennie was quite wealthy when she built the House of Mirrors, there is a wonderful tale surrounding her financing. A story was widely circulated in later years that the police chief from St. Louis decided to assist Jennie in opening her Denver house of ill fame by blackmailing one of Denver's leading citizens. Apparently this man's first wife had pulled a disappearing act, and the gentleman had since married into a wealthy Denver family. Jennie's St. Louis friend and other influential friends began circulating the rumor that the first wife had been murdered. In the dead of night, they even buried the skull of an Indian woman found on the plains in the man's backyard as "proof." Next, the St. Louis officer and two other men called at the man's home posing as investigators, conducted a search, and dug up the skull. The surprised tycoon was innocent, and knew he was so. Nevertheless, such a scandal could ruin his political career. Accordingly, the man "donated" $17,780 for Jennie's new house. The matter was forgotten until it was related years later by someone who remembered the story.[5]

The House of Mirrors quickly became one of the most prominent structures in Denver's red-light district. There were twenty-seven rooms in all, including a kitchen, ballroom, four parlors, a wine room, an indoor bathroom, and sixteen bedrooms upstairs (given the square footage of the building, the sixteen bedrooms likely functioned as small, partitioned cribs). The front parlor featured mirrors from ceiling to floor. Jennie commissioned five stone faces adhered to the facade of the building, including a bust of herself at the top. There has been never-ending speculation about who the other faces represented, including a story that they portrayed those involved in the blackmailing of the rich man who "murdered" his wife. The exterior decor also featured fancy scrollwork in a variety of mysterious designs. Inside were only the best in female employees with style, good looks, and excellent manners. Jennie selected the girls' costumes herself, ordering them from local dressmakers and charging her employees for the cost.

On August 13, 1899, Jennie married John "Jack" Wood, a former bartender at the elite Brown Palace Hotel who now drove a hack. Wood was fourteen years younger than Jennie, but the two seemed to complement one another. Jennie purchased a saloon in Salt Lake City for Wood to run. When she paid him a surprise visit a few months later, however, she found him in the arms of another woman and shot him in the arm. When police asked why she did it, she exclaimed, "I shot him because I love him, damn him!" Jack persuaded authorities to release Jennie.[6] On another occasion, Jennie heard Jack was messing around with one Mollie Gibson at his bar in Omaha, which Jennie also had financed. This time, Jennie summoned Wood to an attorney's office in Omaha and "for nearly an hour the storm raged, and when at last the clouds of battle began to clear away a contract securing to Miss Rogers her financial rights in the business was drawn up and signed, and she returned to Denver."[7]

In 1891 madam Ella Wellington contracted with Jennie to purchase the House of Mirrors. The former wife of Fred Bouse (or Bowse) of Omaha, Ella had forsaken her confining life as a wife and mother of two adopted children and ran off with one Sam Cross. After Cross apparently left her in Salt Lake City, Ella made her way to Denver. She appeared to be doing quite well, even advertising in the 1892 *Denver Red Book*, a guide to the saloons and pleasure resorts around Market Street.

Ella, Jennie, and other Market Street madams were flooded with applications following the Silver Panic of 1893. Numerous young women, maids in particular, suddenly found themselves out of a job as the silver market crashed. Ever mindful of the kind of women she hired, Jennie "is said to have questioned each girl as to her background and moral fiber." Whether she hired any of them is unknown, but she did send "ninety-six girls to respectable boardinghouses until she could pay their expenses back to their hometowns."[8]

Jennie had barely rid herself of her charges when the House of Mirrors came back to her in a most tragic fashion. One evening in 1894, some old friends from Ella Wellington's hometown unexpectedly paid her a visit. Fred was remarried, they said, and the new family was doing just fine. The news was too much for Ella, who abruptly started upstairs exclaiming, "O I am so happy! So happy that I'll just blow my goddam brains out!" Upon reaching her bedroom, Ella did just that. At the time, Arapahoe County clerk William R. Prinn was lying in Ella's bed and later gave his statement to the coroner. Following a funeral procession that took every available carriage in town, Ella was buried at Riverside Cemetery. Her most loyal admirer, Frederick Sturges, spent the next three weeks sleeping on top of her grave. He also purchased a plot next to hers before overdosing on morphine. In his pocket was a picture of Ella with a note written on the back: "Bury this picture of my own dear Ella beside me."[9]

Shortly after taking the House of Mirrors back, Jennie changed the name to "The Stone Front" and advertised it as such in the *Traveler's Night Guide of Colorado*, another directory of the state's pleasure resorts that were "guaranteed strictly first-class and safe (financially and otherwise)." Jennie was still there in 1896 when Jack Wood died in Omaha, of heart disease, on February 28. She had him buried in Evergreen Cemetery with a headstone that read "He is not dead but sleepeth." Perhaps Wood's untimely death made Jennie restless, for she began moving around—to an address on Lawrence Street in 1897, to 2016 Market Street in 1898, and finally to 2020 Market Street in 1899.[10]

The year 1902 proved to quite stressful: Jennie's beloved dog died, and she was diagnosed with Bright's disease. She moved to Chicago and opened another brothel. In her absence, Polly Pry, Denver's favorite

Jennie Rogers was the belle of the ball in Denver until she succumbed to Bright's disease.
Courtesy History Colorado, #PH.PROP.217.

gossip, happened to publish an attack on Mother Jones, the "national labor agitator," in January 1904. Pry claimed the Pinkerton Detective Agency had an entire file on Jones describing her as "a well-known character, not alone in the 'Red Light' district of Denver, but in Omaha, Kansas City, Chicago and San Francisco" back in 1889. One of the documents in the file identified Jones (née Mary Harris) as "an inmate of Jennie Rogers' house on Market Street, Denver, some twelve years ago. She got into trouble with the Rogers woman for bribing all the girls to leave her and go to a house in Omaha for which act she was paid a procuress fee of $5 to $10 apiece for the girls."[11]

If Jennie heard about Polly Pry's column, she may have disregarded it, for she had fallen in love again. Her new man was a contractor named Archibald Fitzgerald, who was even younger than Jennie than Jack Wood had been—twenty years—but Jennie didn't mind. The two were married on April 26, 1904, in Hot Springs, Arkansas. Following a brief trip to Denver for the funeral of prostitute Lizzie Preston, however, Jennie returned to Chicago only to learn that Fitzgerald was still married to two other women. In actuality, Fitzgerald had indeed married both Abbie Lighthall and another woman named Sarah back in 1896 in Chicago. Only the latter woman seems to have filed for divorce, in 1903, claiming Fitzgerald had abandoned her two years earlier.

Jennie left Fitzgerald and returned to Denver in late 1906, taking over management of the House of Mirrors for a time. As unfaithful as he was, however, Fitzgerald remained very much on the madam's mind. On January 1, 1907, she wrote to him at Goldfield, Nevada. "I thought of you many times last night," she said, "and when the New Year Bell at 12 o'clock began to ring I was at the lunch table with the ladys [*sic*] all seated at the table. They all seemed to wish me much joy but little did they know how sad my heart was at that moment. I left the table as soon as I could and went to my room and you know the rest. There were several balls last night and most all the folks on this street were there. I staid [*sic*] home and took in $75.00."¹²

On October 1 Jennie wrote to Fitzgerald again, touching on his infidelity and using stationery from Chicago's Bismark Hotel, where she must have visited recently. "I have been in coart [*sic*] all day and will go to coart at nine o'clock tomorrow morning," she told Fitzgerald. "I think I will win the case. I have four good witnesses . . . I hope you will be good and then I will be happy . . . But if you was to make free with any of them wimon [*sic*] I [would] not care to go back to Hot Springs. I will not take the medison [*sic*], only when it is [necessary]. I feel so blue and so lonesome . . . I know my health is breaking down and worry has done it all. God help me to shut out the past and start a new life. Darling tell me when you return to Hot Springs. Will you be kind and loving as a husband. My heart longs for your love—and if I have not got it I am better [off] to go way where I never will see you . . . When I see what a great change there is in you sense [*sic*] I first met you. I hope Darling you will think this over and write me a long letter. Ever your devoted wife, Jennie."¹³

Jennie and Fitzgerald did reconcile, at least long enough for Jennie to visit him in Arkansas. In about 1908 she moved from the House of Mirrors to a place on Larimer Street, and focused on her favorite parlor house at 1950 Market Street. In May 1909 she made extensive renovations with new light fixtures and furniture repairs, including replacing the mirror on her own dresser. She could afford it, for her girls were paying her $250 per month in rent. The house was quite lavish, consisting of front and back parlors (one in green and one in red), a "Turkish room," a dining room with a table to seat sixteen people, a ballroom, fourteen bedrooms, and a "Front Alcove Room" on the second floor, which also contained a bed. All of the rooms were well furnished with Axminster carpets from England, mahogany and leather-upholstered chairs and couches, lace curtains, artworks, and cuspidors. Three pianos were arranged throughout the house. The bedrooms—some furnished with rocking chairs and writing desks—each had their own commode.[14]

Jennie's health continued to fail, and by October 10 she was at Sisters of Mercy Hospital. From her bed, she summoned her physician, Dr. Hugh L. Taylor, and asked about her condition. Taylor confirmed that the future looked grim. "She said the reason she wanted to know that was if there was any danger she had certain business matters that she wanted to attend to at once," Taylor later said, adding that upon Jennie's request he summoned her attorney, Stanley C. Warner, so she could make out her will.[15] Jennie Rogers, the self-proclaimed "Queen of the Colorado Underworld," died October 17, 1909. She was buried in Denver's Fairmount Cemetery under the name Leah J. Wood, next to Jack Wood. Many of her friends from the demimonde attended the funeral.

Jennie left a sizable estate that included four parlor houses on Market Street and several other properties. Fitzgerald's name was noticeably missing in her will, which named her sister, Annie Smith; her niece, Annie Prestile; and her nephew, Marsh Warner, as heirs. Each was designated to receive one-third of her estate. Fitzgerald filed a protest claiming, among other things, that her name was Leah J. Fitzgerald, not Wood, and that she was of unsound mind when she signed the will. The court initially dismissed Fitzgerald's claim, until he was able to prove his case with a marriage certificate and other documentation. He eventually settled for $5,000 in cash, jewelry, and some property in Illinois.

It took several more months to settle the rest of Jennie's estate, during which time Ella Kelly remained a renter at the 1950 Market Street house. Repairs and deliveries to the house continued as needed. Ella eventually purchased the property, while the House of Mirrors sold to Mattie Silks for $14,000. Mattie had sold Jennie her first house, and now she purchased her last house, bringing the illustrious madam of Market Street's career full circle.

A Violent Femme

———•◦•———

Mollie May of Leadville

L eadville, at the lofty altitude of over 10,000 feet, owed its existence to the early gold camp of Oro City which sprang up in about 1861. Almost immediately gamblers and prostitutes flocked to the camp, conducting business in wagons and tents before buildings were constructed. Oro City faded when local gold deposits waned, but silver veins were discovered in nearby California Gulch and a new town, Leadville, started. The post office opened in 1877 as the sporting ladies and gentlemen of Oro City traipsed over to Leadville.

A local newspaper once called Leadville's dance halls "breathing holes of hell, where customers imbibe torchlight whiskey and indulge in the quadrille and the whirling sinuosity's of the waltz."[1] There were six dance halls within a year, while brothels opened along Harrison Avenue, State Street, West Third and West Fifth Streets, and Chestnut Street. "I seldom go down [there]," wrote Princeton graduate George Elder to his family in those early days, "but when I do I always notice [the dance halls] full and lots of music and noise."[2]

State Street, in the older section of town, was especially noted for having everything from fancy houses of ill repute to lowly cribs, with a mixture of ethnicities and ages. Newly arrived girls as young as fourteen or fifteen who dared wander onto State Street could be "raped and

Early State Street in Leadville was busy with hawkers, merchants, and lustful ladies.
Courtesy Jan MacKell Collins.

forced to work in a bawdy house." By 1878 the activities of the notorious women of Leadville were often commented upon in newspapers
throughout the state as they drank and danced their way through the
demimonde. It was into this raucous mix that Mollie May arrived in
the 1870s. Sometimes known as Jennie, Mollie, or Maggie Mickey, the
woman's story remains in the limelight of Leadville's bawdy history
even today.[3]

Born in 1851 as Milinda or Melinda May Bryant, to Thomas and Bessie Bryant in Virginia, Mollie was said to have lost her virginity to a "lustful suitor" who found her in Illinois, took her to Cheyenne, Wyoming, and dumped her there.[4] With nowhere else to go, Mollie found a job performing for theater owner Jim McDaniels in Cheyenne, doubling as a prostitute. When McDaniels moved his theater to the Blacks Hill of South Dakota in 1876, Mollie went along too. The Black Hills gold rush was just beginning. The infant city of Deadwood was new, and raw, but it also offered lots of opportunity for a girl like Mollie, and she soon opened her own brothel.

Most of Deadwood's whorehouses were situated on the north end of the city along lower Main Street, appropriately called the "Badlands District." Mollie's admirers included Jim May, a local Black Hills freighter whose brother was the notorious bounty hunter Boone May. Both men took a liking to Mollie. In May of 1876, at the Gem Theater, the brothers argued over her. Boone fired a shot at Jim, but hit Mollie instead. Amazingly, the metal in Mollie's corset deflected the bullet, saving her life. Mollie actually preferred Jim, but after the shooting he didn't want anything to do with her. She took his name anyway.[5]

The shooting affair was the first of many scrapes for Mollie. Soon afterward she was involved in a skirmish with prostitute Fannie Garretson. The dispute was over a banjo player, "Banjo" Dick Brown, who married Fannie in November 1876. The couple was united by E. B. Farnum, Deadwood's first mayor. Their deep love, and jealousy, for one another was quite mutual; a few days after the marriage, Brown shot and killed Edward Shaughnessy, with whom Fannie had previously lived. Shortly after that, Mollie, Fannie, and Brown were jaunting along in a closed carriage when the two women began fighting. In the fray, Fannie bit off a chunk of Mollie's ear. Afterward, Mollie wisely decided to leave Deadwood and traveled to Colorado. Her first stops in the Centennial State were Silver Cliff and Bonanza, where she soon became known as the girlfriend of an outlaw named Bill Tripp. She also spent some time in Pueblo, where she became known as the girl of gambler Sam Mickey.[6]

By 1878, Mollie was in Leadville. She staked her first claim in a house on Main Street, which became known as "one of the most imposing residences in the city" and even featured one of the first telephones in town. In about July of 1879, she was summoned to court with several other prostitutes.[7] Notably, the *Leadville Chronicle* described "Miss Molly May" as being "modestly dressed in black." Of the defendants, the newspaper reporter discovered that "neither their dress nor faces gave in evidence that they were women of the town . . . their conduct was, if you please, lady-like."[8]

As she had in Deadwood, Mollie also continued seeing, and being involved in, the violence that was so common in boomtowns like Leadville. In September the *Chronicle* published an article with the headline "Riot at Mollie May's," wherein two men had burst into her parlor house and "tore up the place." Mollie was "knocked down and kicked all around the room. She was very much battered and bruised."[9] Mollie was not herself without fault; in November 1879 she was accused of stealing a necklace from one Mattie Cook.

As Mollie settled into Leadville's demimonde, her old friend Jim McDaniels came to town. He had successfully purchased the Bella Union Theater in Deadwood and had shipped an amazing forty thousand pounds of theater scenery to Leadville. In 1880 he purchased the former New Athenaeum Theater on State Street and renamed it the New Leadville Theater, or McDaniels' Theater. Mollie, meanwhile, sold her house on Main to the city, which used it for the city hall, and moved to 129 West Fifth Street—an address she retained for the rest of her time in Leadville.

On February 14, 1880, Leadville's *Carbonate Chronicle* reported that one James Burns was shot as he crossed some lots on his way to Mollie's. With him was W. F. Vincent, and the two had just left

Spencer's saloon. The shooter was James Langan, who, upon seeing Burns on his property, had shouted, "Don't you cross this lot, you son of a bitch!" before firing. Mollie's housekeeper, Hattie Dickhurst, heard the commotion and found Burns lying on the back porch. He was taken inside and put on a sofa as doctors were summoned, but died as they tried to save him. Langan was inexplicably released on the grounds of self-defense.[10]

Somehow, Mollie managed to persevere through her trials and tribulations as a brothel owner. The 1880 census recorded ten female "boarders" and two male employees at her brothel. Mollie apparently tried to remove herself from the eyes of authorities by using the name Jessie Brown, but was outed by the newspapers when she was brought to court in September and fined seventy-five dollars. Police had staged a raid on four brothels, including Mollie's. In the latter instance, two "nice young men" were seen jumping from Mollie's second-floor window to escape arrest. In court, the women uttered "some unkind words," while the *Carbonate Chronicle* explained the raids were made because the local police "were not on the best terms with the Alderman, on account of delinquent salaries, and they had information . . . that several members of the august body might be found at some of the palaces pulled, and that the license business was only a blind."[11]

Also, Mollie's old enemy, Fannie Garretson Brown, resurfaced. After traveling with Dick Brown during 1878, the couple had separated and Fannie—like many other "Black Hillers" seeking greener pastures—wound up in Leadville. In 1879 she performed at McDaniels' Theater but left soon after; she does not appear in census records or city directories after 1880. How Mollie felt about Fannie's appearance in Leadville remains unrecorded, but surely she must have felt at least a hint of superiority now that she was a madam, even as her injured ear ached.

Leadville's "lengthy calendar of crime" continued, often in the vicinity of, if not at, Mollie May's parlor house. On an afternoon in November, shots were heard coming from the red-light district. Police arrived to find miner Lewis Lamb lying in the snow in front of the bordello of Winnie Purdy. Former marshal Martin Duggan, a bully Lamb had known from childhood, was standing over the body. Duggan willingly handed his pistol over to officers, saying "I am the man that done it." The *Leadville Daily Herald* reported the men got into an argument, which started when Duggan almost ran over Lewis with a sleigh he was delivering to Winnie's. Duggan claimed Lewis drew a gun on him a few minutes later. In the ensuing fracas, Duggan said he dove behind the horses hitched to the sleigh and shot Lamb in self-defense.[12]

Mindy Lamb, Lewis's wife, swore revenge on Duggan, promising him, "I shall wear black and mourn this killing until the very day of your death and then, Goddam you, I will dance upon your grave." The quote was widely circulated, and a few days later, Mollie stopped Mindy on the street. "You don't know me," she told Mindy, "but I wanted to tell you that what happened to a decent man like your husband was a dirty rotten shame and I'm really sorry for you." The two women remained friends, often having a chat directly in front of Mollie's parlor house. Rare was an open friendship between respectable housewives and ladies of the evening.[13]

Mollie and her colleagues continued experiencing troubles throughout 1881. In February prostitute Kittie Sheedy got into a knife fight with one of Mollie's girls, Lou Ward. The fight began outside, but Kittie actually chased Lou into the brothel, where she was slashed several times before Mollie managed to break the women up. Mollie also had her adversaries, the most notable one being Sally Purple, who owned the brothel next door. Once, after shouting insults at each other from their respective houses, the women actually began firing guns at one another. The battle ended two hours later with no injuries. "Both parties are resting on their arms," chortled the *Leadville Democrat*, "and awaiting daybreak to resume hostilities."[14]

By 1882 Mollie had acquired a second brothel at 131 West Fifth Street. Later that year, she charged Annie Layton with stealing a dress. The argument escalated in court when Annie accused Mollie of running a house of ill fame, and Mollie retaliated by revealing that Annie was employed as a prostitute. Ultimately, all charges were dropped. Of much more importance to the public, however, was Mollie's taking in of a three-year-old child. "It was no more than a bargain sale," reported Pueblo's *Daily Chieftain* in May of 1882, "the Cyprian paying the parents so much money for the child and they signing an indenture for its adoption. The indignation is great, but just what steps will be taken in the matter is not fully determined."[15]

The *Chieftain* also had something to say about the morals of Leadville's respectable citizens who "allowed a helpless, sinless child to be abused, kicked, cursed, persecuted and starved by its brutal parents without lifting a hand to save [it] until a woman of the town came forward and took the little one under her protection."[16] The madam herself stayed silent until a local newspaper voiced concerns about her intentions. In May, Mollie contacted the *Leadville Herald* and gave an exclusive interview, explaining that the child belonged to a decent woman who was too poor to care for her. Mollie was caring for the baby until the mother could contact relatives for assistance. She ended the interview by angrily reminding the general public of all the charities she made donations to on a regular basis. In the end, the mother never reclaimed her child and Mollie adopted her. She was called Ella Moore, even though Mollie said the Moores were not the child's parents.

Mollie's odd habit of taking in wayward children continued. In June 1884 the *Carbonate Chronicle* reported that she had returned from a trip to Utah with "a brown-eyed, yellow haired little girl scarcely three years old." Mollie said she had met the child and her mother on the train, the latter explaining that she broke up with her Mormon husband when he brought a new wife home. The woman had appealed to her parents for shelter, but they refused to take the child in with her. She was on her way to deposit the girl with the state asylum when Mollie met her. Mollie, "attracted by the beauty of the child," offered to take her and the mother "willingly placed it in her care." Back in Leadville, Mollie's housekeeper, Laura Graham, expressed her desire to adopt the child.[17]

In August the *Leadville Daily Herald* revealed that the little girl had actually already been adopted by a woman in Green River, Wyoming, when Mollie met her on the train. The unnamed women had "concluded that she did not want a child as badly as she thought she did" and was taking her to a poorhouse or asylum when Mollie offered to take the toddler. As for Laura Graham, she too tired of caring for the girl and had passed her on to a Leadville laundress. In this fashion, the girl was passed around quite a bit before finally being officially adopted by a respectable couple in town.[18] As for Ella Moore, she was sent off to St. Scholastica's Institute in Highland, Illinois. Her guardian was listed as one Robert Buck.

In between the children she took in, Mollie struggled with her continuing troubles in the red-light district. In March of 1884 she accidentally left her $500 sealskin coat at the brothel of Lillie Saunders. Upon returning for it the next morning, Mollie found the coat had been "literally cut to pieces."[19] And in August, just after the scandal about the three-year-old child had surfaced, another customer "abused" one of her girls and wrecked her house.[20]

Mollie needed a break. The 1885 Colorado census found her in the fledgling town of Pitkin, living near other prostitutes. As she had in the 1880 census, Mollie told the census taker that she had been born in Virginia, her father was born in Germany, and her mother was born in Ireland. She also said she was divorced. Three other women in Mollie's house—Annie Holmes, Mattie Hughes, and Annie Winds— were between twenty-five and thirty-two years of age. Not surprisingly,

Annie Holmes's three-year-old son, Frank, also lived there. Children, it seemed, could always find shelter with the kindhearted Mollie May.

Just a month after the census was taken, Mollie received word that the woman running her Leadville house "skipped out with $700 or $800 of Mollie's money." Mollie notified the nearest sheriff, at Buena Vista, but the thief was probably never caught. Pitkin, meanwhile, wasn't amounting to much anyway, and Mollie returned to Leadville. But it was no better; in February 1886 yet another customer wreaked havoc at Mollie's house. In March Mollie argued with three men in her brothel, and when she tried to blow the police whistle she kept in her pocket, "one of the men held her mouth while another one of them struck her in the face." Later that month, Mollie got in a fistfight with Mollie Price, but was released without charges.[21]

Mollie May died on April 13, 1887, from what the *Leadville Weekly Chronicle* called "neuralgia of the heart." She was only thirty-six years old, but years of rough living must have caught up with her. Her funeral was one of the largest processions in Leadville, and even Mindy Lamb insisted on attending. The services took place in Mollie's brothel before a $3,000 hearse and eight carriages accompanied her body to Leadville's Evergreen Cemetery. Her obituary, circulated as far away as Pueblo, stated, "She was a woman who, with all her bad qualities, was much given to charity and was always willing to help the poor and unfortunate."[22]

J. H. Monheimer was appointed executor of Mollie's estate, which was valued at $25,000 and included her property, cash, and her $8,000 diamond collection. Her personal property sold for $1,500, and her house was occupied by prostitute Jenni Lester until it was purchased by one Anna Ferguson for $3,600. Newspapers speculated the money would go to six-year-old Ella Moore, who was confirmed as "attending one of the schools in the east," and that "the foster mother idolized the child and her life was wrapped up in its future." After her schooling, Ella Moore returned to Leadville. In 1901 the *Leadville Herald* published an article about twenty-year-old "Lillian" Moore, adopted daughter of Mollie May, who attempted suicide in Leadville. Doctors saved her life and she was last seen on a train headed to Denver, where, like so many others, she disappeared without a trace.[23]

A FAMILY AFFAIR

———◄●►———

*The Vanolis of the
San Juan Mining Camps*

As Colorado's gold and silver booms extended into the 1870s, rich strikes in the San Juan Mountains resulted in a number of mining camps. Some of them—namely Ouray, Telluride, and Silverton—grew to be large municipalities with schools and churches. Nestled in between these sanctimonious places were saloons, gambling dens, dance halls, and brothels. The latter were in such abundance that it is no wonder that the three towns gained reputations for being wild and woolly. The first in this trilogy of towns, Silverton, opened its post office on February 1, 1875. Ouray followed on October 28, and Telluride would be founded in 1878. In just a few short years, all three towns would experience massive growth as thousands of prospectors poured into the San Juans.

Naturally, the three boomtowns were an ideal place for the prostitution industry to flourish, which it did with much vigor. Greene Street in Silverton, Main Street in Ouray, and Pacific Avenue in Telluride each featured everything from two-room cribs to grand parlor houses, plus dance halls where bawdy entertainment could include anything from dance-hall floozies to musical shows. These pleasant diversions soon numbered in the dozens. A man needed only to access a number of trails and travel a day or so to reach any one of the towns in the San

Juan Mountains' triangle of love for sale. Notably, Ouray was one of the only towns in the San Juans to have documented prostitutes in the 1880 census. Their statistics are interesting: Their average age was 24.5 years, and roughly one-third of them were married, widowed, or divorced.

Beginning in about 1881, society at large began noticing the size of the red-light districts and speculated whether or not such places were good for the population. In its August 20 edition, the *Ouray Times* commented, "If a dance hall is well managed, and kept in a proper place, and the prostitutes are not allowed to parade the streets and back alleys, we see no reasonable grounds for complaint, but when they get to scattering here and there, and use vulgar and obscene language, it is high time that there should be some action taken to stop such nuisances. Fire them out."[1]

Indeed, the dance halls and red-light districts were growing, sometimes out of control, and even more so after the Denver and Rio Grande Railroad reached the San Juan region beginning in 1882. Various ordinances and subsequent arrests started taking place, with newspapers scrambling to keep up with each occurrence. Most of the efforts were for naught; the authorities were no match for the hundreds of shady ladies, brothel owners, and saloon men who infiltrated Ouray, Silverton, and Telluride.

The history of the red-light districts of the San Juans might have been quite different but for a most unique occurrence that transpired beginning in 1884. As writer Robert L. Brown put it, "the underworld gained control of Silverton and ran the town from their dens on Blair Street." Accordingly, vigilante groups were formed in an attempt to restore order, as city authorities sent for none other than Bat Masterson of notorious Dodge City in Kansas. Masterson was duly hired as police chief and at least managed to calm things down.[2] Brown was no doubt referring to a number of large Italian families who moved to the San Juans and soon owned numerous saloons, gambling dens, and dance halls. Italian overlords were certainly immigrating to far-off places like New York, where their numbers grew from a mere 20,000 to 250,000 between 1880 and 1890. In frontier Colorado, however, the presence of such factions was virtually unknown.

The best-known Italian family in the San Juans was the Vanoli family, who were far from typical of brothel owners in other places throughout the state. For over thirty years, the family reigned as one of the most respected in Ouray, Silverton, and Telluride. Not only did they openly advertise their businesses in local newspapers, but they also regularly participated in citywide celebrations, invested in mines, made and kept numerous friends, maintained a camaraderie with their fellow Italians, took care of their ailing and aged customers and friends, contributed to fund-raisers, and joined local lodges. Newspapers reported on their activities in social columns, congratulated them on their successes, and mourned them when they died. The Vanolis were indeed just like any other large Italian family—the exception being that saloons, dance halls, and red-light women were their line of business.

The story of the Vanoli family begins with brothers John and Dominick Vanoli, who came to Ouray in about 1884. John purchased property in the red-light district along Main Street, north of Eighth Avenue. With Dominick as his partner, he opened the Gold Belt Theater as well as several brothels. The Gold Belt featured entertainment on the first floor, with cribs on the second floor. John also purchased the Grand Pacific Hotel and converted it to the "220 Club," another dance hall that was sometimes known as a "boarding house." John, his family, and their employees appear to have been working-class citizens who catered to working-class customers. In time, however, the Vanolis would experience great wealth and respect.[3]

The Gold Belt Theater in particular became known as a "first class vaudeville theater." At the center of the entertainment was a beautiful piano made by the William Bourne Piano Company in 1882, which was installed in the theater shortly after it opened. First-rate musicals took place at the Gold Belt, and customers imbibed freely at the bar while playing cards and other games of chance. The Vanolis were so good about paying their business taxes that the theater and its naughty environs went unmolested. Indeed, John Vanoli worked to "self-police" his own businesses.[4]

Other brothels, saloons, and gambling dens might experience run-ins with the law, but the Vanoli properties took care of their own. They first made the newspapers on June 4, 1886, when it was reported that "John Vanoli was assaulted by Samuel Starr with a six-shooter Tuesday morning." The incident merited no more than two sentences, but the power of the Vanoli boys is strongly inferred by the closing comment that "Starr is one of those would-be bad men who will be grid-ironed the next time he shows up in Ouray."[5] By the time the Denver and Rio Grande rails reached Ouray in 1887, the Vanolis owned the Gold Belt, the 220 Club, a restaurant, two saloons, a Chinese laundry, and a livery stable.

Unfortunately, even the powerful Vanoli brothers were sometimes helpless to prevent violence in their businesses. In 1887 a fiddler from the 220 became enamored with one of the girls. When the woman spurned his advances, the man followed her to a boardinghouse, punched a hole in the window, and shot her. The culprit "was caught literally red-handed with his arm stuck in the windowpane."[6] A year later, John Vanoli was working behind the bar at the 220 when a "burro man" identified as Sam Bass, or Best, came in. Bass turned his revolver over to Vanoli, an act that may have been a house rule, and spent the next several hours dancing and drinking. Later in the evening the inebriated man went to the bar, retrieved his gun, and was on his way out the door when a girl enticed him into one more dance. This time Bass got into a fight with one Jack Dugan. Bass struck Dugan over the head with his revolver, followed him to the bar, and hit him again. Vanoli pulled his own gun and shot Bass. The man was taken to the hospital and later died.

What happened next makes an interesting commentary on the Vanolis' reputation in Ouray: "Vanoli who did the shooting was looking
around for quite twenty-four hours trying to give himself up," reported
the *Ouray Solid Muldoon*, "but no one seemed disposed to take him
in and he might have been wandering about yet if the county attorney
had not made a complaint, and he was finally jailed."[7] Vanoli duly went
to court and eventually was sentenced to two years in the state penitentiary beginning in May 1889. In July the *Solid Muldoon* suggested
circulating a petition to free the man. Several persons, including the
district attorney and the sheriff, signed the petition, and Vanoli was
pardoned in December.

The Vanolis' reputations were not only secured in Ouray, but also
in Telluride, Silverton, and even the budding camp of Red Mountain
between Ouray and Silverton. There, in 1892, John Vanoli paid $12.50
in taxes. He also was exonerated once again in April of 1895 when he
killed yet another man. This time, Vanoli was asleep when he heard
gunshots at the Gold Belt Theater. The perpetrator was one Ed Leggett,
who was shooting up the hall. Rousting himself out of bed, Vanoli "came
in and shot" Leggett, who was not expected to live. Vanoli once again
"gave himself up" and was apparently pardoned once more, for there is
no further news of his arrest or subsequent jail time.[8]

There is a chance that John Vanoli was spared jail time because he
was ill. By December, he "was in the last stages of consumption and was
told he could only live a few weeks longer at the utmost." Vanoli began
traveling, eventually visiting the home of his friend, one A. Baccilieri in
Oakland, California, where he spent Christmas. On December 27 he
was taken ill and confined to bed. Doctors were summoned but couldn't
be of much assistance. That evening, Vanoli asked for a pen and paper
so he could make out his will. Baccilieri supplied the materials and left
the room. For reasons known only to himself, however, Vanoli committed suicide by gunshot before making the will. His expansive estate

included two theaters, one in Ouray and one in Trinidad, plus property in Denver, Salt Lake City, and other places.[9]

Dominick Vanoli eventually opened the Gold Belt Branch Dance Hall in Telluride, offering premium entertainment and running advertisements for the place for the next several years. Partnering with him now were his children: Tony, Barney, Minnie, and Mary. Tony in particular appeared in the newspapers often as they commented on his comings and goings. "Tony Vanoli returned [to Ouray] from Telluride Wednesday where he is running a show," reported the *Telluride Daily Journal* in 1899, for example. "He contemplates playing a part of his troupe here."[10] His household in the 1900 census included himself, brother Barney, and sister "Domerica" (Mary), as well as two bartenders and a boarder. Tony was now thirty years old and listed as running a saloon. Mary, whose occupation was left blank, was twenty-three years old. Eighteen-year-old Barney was attending school.

In the meantime, Dominick's wife, Maria, finally emigrated from Italy to be with her husband in Ouray in 1901. Just a year later, however, she died from typhoid fever. In spite of being a virtual newcomer in town, Maria had the family Vanoli backing her and was already regarded as "a woman beloved and respected by many friends [whose] loss is sincerely mourned by them." Maria's funeral was quite large, with lots of flowers, and services were conducted for her at the Catholic church.[11]

In 1904 the Vanolis were still in power, as illustrated by an incident in which an "itinerant cook by the name of Harnett struck town one day this week, got loaded up on fighting whiskey and attempted to whip all the sons of Italy in Vanoli's saloon" at Ouray. Harnett landed in jail instead, paying a twenty-dollar fine.[12] Times, however, were changing. In February of 1906 the *Telluride Journal* reported on Viola Peterson, a habitué of Dominick's Gold Belt Branch Dance Hall, who had died at a local boardinghouse. Viola was but sixteen years of age and had run away from Sweden as a very young girl. Following her arrival in New

York City, she had come West with a performing troupe called the Liberty Bells. At Denver Viola left the group and made her way to Telluride, where she began working at the Gold Belt Branch and subsequently contracted a venereal disease.

Viola told her doctor before she died that she had no idea what the dance hall really was and had been told it was simply a place of amusement. Having arrived in town with no money or friends, taking work at the Gold Belt Branch had been the only way Viola could make a living. "How a man born in the image of his maker could seduce a mere girl and have her take up a life of this kind is a mystery," scolded the paper. "It's a wonder he was not stricken dead for the act." Although the paper neglected to mention who the man was, an invisible finger seemed to point at Dominick Vanoli. A collection was taken up by Viola's friends and she was buried at Lone Tree Cemetery.[13]

As of 1908, the Vanoli holdings in Ouray were still strong. Among their businesses along Main Street were the Gold Belt Theater, the 220 Club, and the Roma Saloon. All three were nestled in the large red-light district, whose "'sin businesses' generated substantial revenue for the town."[14] The Ouray businesses were still a family affair; the 1910 census finds Dominick living with Barney while the two operated a saloon. Mary and Minnie lived in the house as well. Next door, madam Ada Hoyt ran a dance hall.

Shortly after the census was taken, Dominick died, and his children continued running the businesses. The Vanoli clan began experiencing a series of troubles that eventually led to the family's downfall beginning in 1911. In April the second Gold Belt in Telluride burned after a fire started on second floor. Two "inmates" were rescued, as well as "four well-known dogs and some kittens." A great number of townspeople lamented the loss of "one of the landmarks of Telluride," regarded as "still a well-known resort." One news story explained that "old residents remember seeing some splendid shows there, with the prices sky high,

Ouray as it appeared in 1908 shows the red-light district intermingled with respectable businesses.
Courtesy Jan MacKell Collins.

with drinks served in the boxes at twenty five and fifty cents each, and the waiters kept busy." Tony Vanoli promised he would soon reopen the theater "in the first floor of the building destroyed by fire yesterday."[15]

Unfortunately, however, the family had become divided over Dominick's estate, at least for a time. When Minnie didn't receive her portion as promised, she sent one Fred Scala to accost Barney about the situation. Barney, the paper reported, knocked Scala out flat. This time, the *Ouray Plaindealer* made light of the situation, writing about the incident tongue in cheek as it would a sporting event.[16]

Over in Telluride, a heated city council meeting in July of 1915 saw angry citizens lodging complaints against the red-light district. After a shouting match between the mayor and chief of police, it was decided to place the matter in the hands of the fire and police board. The *Telluride Daily Journal* predicted that in doing so, "this said vicious character will no doubt pack her duds and leave for other parts within a very short time."[17] In the following months, nobody escaped persecution. Women of the town were brought to court and paid steep fines. In 1916 action was taken to close Telluride's remaining six brothels, as well as some houses outside the district. This time, six brothel owners were served with papers. Papers were even taken to Ouray and served on Minnie Vanoli, who ran her brothel in Telluride. But the officers were merely carrying through on a new state law prohibiting prostitution, which had been passed by the legislature the year before.

Hard evidence of the economic hardships suffered by the Vanoli family comes from a 1919 list of delinquent taxes, on which Mary Vanoli appeared. Mary had actually been suffering from some mental health issues as early as 1915, when she accompanied Sheriff E. A. Krisher from Pueblo to Ouray. Mary, it was noted, "has been taking treatment in Dr. Week's sanitarium for the past several months."[18] By 1920 Mary was living in the now-defunct Roma Saloon in Ouray. Next door to her, presumably in one of the other formerly glorious Vanoli businesses, were Minnie and Barney. The census documented Minnie as keeping a lodging house. Shortly after the census was taken, Mary was declared "insane" and "spent two stints in the Pueblo Insane Asylum."[19]

Mary was back in Ouray by the time of the 1930 census, living with Minnie and Barney. Of the three, only Barney was employed, as a miner. A single boarder, Anton Schrinard, lived with the Vanolis. The following year, Barney Vanoli died and was buried with other family members in Ouray's Cedar Hill Cemetery.

By 1940 Prohibition had been repealed, and Minnie opened a beer hall in the old Roma Saloon. The hall was commonly known as "Minnie's Place," and Minnie and Mary lived upstairs. But it was hardly the same as the halcyon days when the Vanoli clan virtually ran the red-light district of Ouray. Still, Minnie kept the old 220 "in pristine condition and ready to open at any moment until her age made it difficult to keep up the establishment." Unfortunately, the old 220 never was revived, and both Minnie and Mary died in 1967. Their passing was the official end of a most historic era in Ouray's red-light history.[20]

LAURA BELL MCDANIEL

— • • —

Queen of the Colorado City Tenderloin

The "Pikes Peak Gold Rush" of 1859 quickly became identifiable with the gold, and other rich minerals, Colorado had to offer. At the base of Pikes Peak itself was an old Ute trail which eventually led travelers to the goldfields in the western portion of the territory. Here, Colorado City sprouted as a supply town for prospectors on their way to the goldfields. The fledgling town suffered troubles almost from the minute it was founded. It was initially made the territorial capital, but more welcoming quarters were soon found in Denver. Both the Civil War and local Indian troubles caused a decline at Colorado City as travelers sought safer routes. The struggling town suffered another blow when Colorado Springs was established nearby in 1871, but soon found an intriguing catch: The new city prohibited gambling, prostitution, and saloons within its city limits. All three sins were available in Colorado City, and the premiere of the Colorado Midland Railroad in 1883 was a great boost to the local economy.

As the population increased, so did the number of saloons and gambling houses along the main drag of Colorado Avenue. The first clue that Colorado City had already objected to the bawds working along Colorado Avenue appeared in May 1888. Following a petition submitted by 250 respected ladies of the town, the Colorado City town board closed down "two 'vile resort' dance halls."[1] But it was too late. A bevy of soiled doves were already flocking to town, dollar signs in their eyes. Among them was Laura Bell McDaniel, destined to reign in Colorado City for thirty years.

Laura Bell's story is unique for a number of reasons. She brazenly defied authorities and remained extremely devoted to her family in a time when the majority of prostitutes were shunned by theirs. She was also a most astute businesswoman, literally setting herself apart from the rest of Colorado City's more common red-light district. She also is the only known madam in Colorado's history who may have met her end at the hands of the authorities when she outright refused to obey the law.

Laura Bell was born to James Monroe and Annie Elizabeth Horton in Buffaloe Lick Township, Missouri. Her brother, James Jr., was born in 1858, and Laura Bell followed in 1861. Following a stint in the Civil War, James Sr. and Annie continued farming and paid an itinerant teacher for "schooling" the children. All was not well, however; in October 1873 Annie visited the Chariton County Court, where she claimed that James "is a person of unsound mind and uncapable of managing his affairs, and prays the court that an inquiry therewith be had as early as possible." James was taken away, eventually landing in the Missouri State Lunatic Asylum at Fulton.[2]

By 1873 the Horton farm was in debt and was subsequently sold. Roughly three years later, Annie Horton divorced her husband and married another farmer, John Warmoth. Of this union came another child, Birdie May, in 1878. Two years later, Laura Bell received the final payment from the farm's sale in the amount of $97.73. With this dowry in hand, she married Samuel Dale in Saline County on November 30, 1880. The marriage proved unsuccessful. In about 1882 Laura Bell left Missouri, presumably without her husband, and here begins one of several colorful tales about her.

Most historians agree that Laura Bell passed through Las Cruces, New Mexico, or El Paso, Texas, where she met R. W. McCarty, better known as "Dusty." The two became lifelong friends. Dusty's cousin was Henry McCarty, alias Billy the Kid, and Laura Bell chanced to meet the famous outlaw. Nothing else is known of Laura Bell's trip, however, until she landed in Salida, Colorado. Salida was founded in 1880 as a division point for the Denver and Rio Grande Railroad. Laura Bell's only child, Eva Pearl Dale, was born there on November 5, 1882.

By 1885 Annie Warmouth was widowed and had joined Laura Bell in Salida, working as a laundress. Laura Bell, who had divorced Sam Dale, worked as a clerk. Annie, Laura Bell, Eva Pearl, and Birdie resided together, along with a nine-year-old nephew named Wiley Short. All seemed well until Laura Bell met up with a local liquor dealer named John Thomas McDaniel, whom she married on April 7, 1887. Barely a month later, while the couple was on a trip to Leadville, the McDaniels' house burned to the ground.

The McDaniels relocated to a new home near the heart of Salida's red-light district. Fires happened all the time in frontier Colorado, and nothing seemed out of place—at first. Later, however, Salida's *Semi-Weekly Mail* newspaper would point out that "the goods in the house were very highly insured" and "circumstances strongly point to Morgan Dunn as the man who fired the building."[3] Dunn was no angel, having spent time in the Colorado State Penitentiary for grand larceny back in 1883. His rough lifestyle was evident from several scars on his head and face, as well as a "gunshot wound" to the right elbow.[4]

Certainly Laura Bell was not expecting what happened next. The date, ominously enough, was Friday the 13th of May 1887. The McDaniels had gone to Annie's house to say good-bye before leaving on a trip to Red Cliff. Dunn, who boarded at Annie's home, was eating dinner when the McDaniels walked in. According to the *Semi-Weekly Mail*, Dunn "commenced abusing" Tom McDaniel. At issue was Dunn's

Laura Bell McDaniel was twenty-six years old when she married Tom McDaniel.
Courtesy Jan MacKell Collins.

feeling that he hadn't been paid enough money for his part in the insurance scheme. At Laura Bell's suggestion, she, Tom, and Annie went to the McDaniels' house. Later that evening, when McDaniel returned from buying candles, he found Dunn in his living room. Dunn resumed his abusive behavior, finally stating, "We're all three here alone and we might as well settle it now as any time."[5]

When Dunn placed his hand menacingly on his hip pocket, McDaniel drew a gun and shot the man five times, "two taking effect with fatal results." Next door at the Arlington Hotel, employees heard the shots and ran to the house. McDaniel, they said, was "standing in front of the door with the two women clinging to him and screaming murder." Annie was shouting, "Oh Tom! Oh Tom! Why did you do that?" to which McDaniel replied, "He had no business in my house." A coroner's jury pored over the evidence concerning the killing of Dunn for three days. Their verdict was "death at the hands of Tom McDaniels [*sic*] without malicious intent, or words to that effect." The *Semi-Weekly Mail* expressed a very different opinion on the matter, hinting that "it is evident that the conservative part of the town are dissatisfied with the work of the coroner's jury in the McDaniels case."[6]

Other questions were posed by the paper, as well as the opinion that "J. M. Lawrence, a worthless lawyer and a man who is insensible to shame, hung the coroner's jury and forced them to exonerate McDaniels of all blame." The paper also revealed that on the afternoon of the shooting, Dunn had "entered the McDaniels house expecting to see Mrs. Warmoth" but encountered Laura Bell instead, whom he then tried to kiss. When Laura Bell told Tom McDaniel about it, his response was, "Why didn't you kill the son of a bitch?" The article concluded that the "murder was a most cold-blooded one without show of reason . . . He was shot to keep his mouth shut. That is all."[7]

Laura Bell wisely decided to leave town, without her husband. She fled to Colorado City and was possibly there by September 12, when her mother married John Kistler. A Civil War veteran, Kistler had owned property in Salida as early as 1884 and presumably met Annie there. That he willfully relocated with Laura Bell's family during such a tumultuous time speaks volumes about his integrity. Furthermore, the Kistlers moved to a house on Grand Avenue (now Vermijo Avenue) close to Laura Bell, whose first quarters were on Colorado Avenue.

By the time Laura Bell came to Colorado City, the population had increased dramatically, from 400 in 1887 to 1,300 in 1888. The north side of Colorado Avenue housed banks, restaurants, and shops. Businesses across the street consisted mostly of saloons. Whether Laura Bell first worked as a prostitute remains unknown, but she must have been studying the industry with vigor. Her ultimate plan was sheer genius:

Rather than remain on Colorado Avenue with the other harlots, Laura Bell chose a house on Grand Avenue two blocks south. Next door was a fabulously large beer garden, complete with a dance pavilion, on West Street (now 25th Street) between Grand Avenue to the south and Washington Avenue (now Cucharras Street) to the north. The Denver and Rio Grande tracks on Washington ran right by the beer garden, allowing passengers to see the entertainments awaiting them.

Laura Bell named her place "The Trilby" after the stylish hats worn by wealthy men of the day. The Trilby had sole access to, or at least first choice of, the male customers from the beer garden. Her first documented employees were probably Belle Barlow and Fernie Brooks, the only two women to appear on Grand Avenue in the 1890 directory. Many historians have asserted that outlaw Jesse James's killer, Bob Ford, dealt faro at Laura Bell's shortly before he was murdered in Creede. In 1891 Laura Bell made the papers the first time after one of her employees, Clara, attempted suicide by morphine.

When a new gold boom occurred in the Cripple Creek mining district on the back of Pikes Peak from Colorado City, the town benefited greatly from the prospectors making their way up Ute Pass. Everyone was making wads of cash, and the Trilby was no exception. Laura Bell was gaining notoriety, as well as a bevy of interesting friends. One of them was John "Prairie Dog" O'Byrne, a colorful hack driver who ran a taxi between Colorado Springs and Colorado City. The passengers loved listening to O'Byrne's stories about the history of the region as they rode along in his wagon, pulled by two tame elk and containing a cage housing a pet prairie dog.

O'Byrne and Laura Bell struck up a special friendship. In about May of 1893, the pair traveled to the World's Columbian Exposition in Chicago. There, one of the elk escaped as O'Byrne was turning them in at a barn for the night. O'Byrne went searching for it in vain, but a local boy was able to capture the animal after a policeman gave up. Afterward, O'Byrne sold the elk to Wild West showman Pawnee Bill in Philadelphia.

Upon her return to Colorado, Laura Bell finally filed for divorce from Tom McDaniel. More might be known of her whereabouts had the local city directory not declined to list known prostitutes beginning in 1894. Only the Kistlers appear in the directory that year, living on Grand Avenue, barely a block from the Trilby. Newspapers, meanwhile, were busy pouncing on the red-light district. "Of all the places to be deplored in this city, the bawdy house is the worst," the *Colorado City Iris* commented in 1896. "There the children of respectable parentage are enticed and their lives forever blighted."[8]

The *Iris* would know, being located on Colorado Avenue between Fifth and Sixth Streets. Had the editors had any inkling that Laura Bell's own daughter was being raised very near the red-light district by the Kistlers, they might have had something even more malicious to say. There is, unfortunately, no evidence showing whether or not the teen-aged Eva Pearl knew what her mother did for a living. Perhaps that is why Laura Bell chose to send Eva Pearl, as "Pearl McDaniel", to the Ursuline Academy, a Catholic convent in Galveston, Texas in about 1896. What the *Iris* didn't know, or chose not to acknowledge, was that Laura Bell was deeply devoted to her family. In February 1898, she witnessed the marriage of Birdie to Edward Moats. When John Kistler died around the same time, Laura Bell no doubt helped her mother apply for his Civil War benefits, as well as his tombstone. By the time city directories began including denizens of the red-light district again in 1899, Laura Bell, her mother, and Birdie and Ed Moats all maintained separate addresses in a one-block area along Grand.

The 1900 census is most telling about Laura Bell's life. The Trilby remained at 419 Grand Avenue, although in the interest of discretion, Laura Bell told the census taker she was an unemployed "landlady."

Two female boarders, Edith Simmons and Maud Ivers, listed their occupations as a milliner and "typewriter," respectively. Two black servants, Sarah Watson and Margaret Scott, also lived in the house. Notably, two men were recorded by the census as well: a stonemason named Patrick Delea and a wholesale liquor dealer named Jake Goldsen. Given that both men were listed as "lodgers" and had no obvious relation to Laura Bell, they may very well have been customers.[9]

Just a few doors down, the census listed Ed and Birdie Moats, as well as Annie Kistler, who worked as a seamstress. Also present was the Moats' newborn son, Cecil. Eva Pearl returned from school in mid-June; although local papers said nothing about it, the June 22, 1900, edition of the *Liberty Vindicator* in Texas announced that "Miss Pearl McDaniel of Colorado Springs, Colorado" had graduated from Ursuline Academy. Fortunately, the girl missed the great hurricane that hit in September, demolishing a large portion of the academy.[10]

Back in Colorado, the 1900 census also verifies that numerous prostitutes had relocated to Washington Avenue in recent years. Colorado City's newly formed red-light district now included three brothels run by madams Nellie Jones, Laura White, and Sadie Stewart. Several other women, working alone or in pairs, are identified by the city directory on the north side of Washington Avenue between Sixth and Seventh Streets. Meanwhile, the beer garden next to the Trilby was losing its shine and would be closed by 1902. Laura Bell wisely decided to move in 1901 to 609 Washington Avenue.

She relocated just in time. Her competitors now included a large bordello at 615 Washington, run by Mamie Majors, who employed seven women. Another brothel at 621 Washington featured five women, and several other prostitutes were available in smaller houses and cribs. Laura Bell clearly had her work cut out for her, but she did it with flair. Within a year, the new Trilby had been expanded to the corner of Washington and Sixth, boldly in clear view of the city hall and jail directly across the street. The old Trilby was added onto and converted into a boardinghouse, while a few doors down, Annie Kistler and Eva Pearl continued sharing the family home. By 1903 Eva Pearl had moved into the old Trilby. Meanwhile, Laura Bell and several other women were arrested for prostitution in April. Laura Bell was charged $500.

Laura Bell's hands were clearly full, dealing with authorities and her business, when Eva Pearl appears to have pulled some sort of shenanigans: In June, she married one Arthur Langdon in Colorado City. The marriage would not have proven so unusual had Eva Pearl not stated her name was "Mary Margaret" on her marriage application.[11] Was she acting out against her mother for sending her to a Catholic school while keeping her own profession a secret? The answer remains unknown as does how Laura Bell felt about Eva Pearl's little joke.

Equally mystifying is why the 1904–5 city directory lists an Edward L. McDaniels living among the girls at the Trilby. What is known is that Laura Bell next set her sights on Cripple Creek and began making trips to the booming city. The madam first boarded at the respectable Waldorf House on South Fourth Street. Next, she began studying bawdy Myers Avenue and its sizable red-light district. Left behind to run her Colorado City parlor house were Rose Healey, Jeanette St. Clair, Clara Stillwell, and cook Margaret Scott.

It could not have been easy for Laura Bell to manage her business affairs in two different towns. Further complicating the situation was her sister Birdie's divorce in February 1905. Ed Moats filed for the divorce on the grounds that Birdie was "not a fit person to have the custody of [their] little son on account of alleged immoral associates."[12] Everybody in the family, and probably in the courts, knew who those "immoral associates" were. And, Birdie didn't help matters when she took Cecil and "skipped to the coast with him" for several months before surfacing in Cripple Creek, where she was immediately arrested for kidnapping her own child.[13]

Birdie settled in Cripple Creek after she remarried to Harry Hooyer in late 1905. When Annie Kistler died in October, Birdie and Laura Bell returned to Colorado City together to oversee their mother's funeral. Laura Bell remained in Colorado City, employing prostitutes Marie French and Lola Siggars, as well as her faithful cook, Margaret Scott. By early 1906, however, she had departed for Cripple Creek once more.

Laura Bell had good reason to leave Colorado City. Beginning in February, local newspapers editorialized how unfair it was that saloons had to pay for liquor licenses while "seven places of prostitution on the row" were selling liquor "without a city license."[14] Another article complained that although the brothels were paying monthly fines, they "should be at least doubled at each appearance of the bawdy house inmates in court, and a jail sentence should be tacked on."[15] During another tirade regarding saloons being required to be closed on Sundays, the *Iris* logically concluded that "the closing of the saloons and billiard and pool halls on Sunday will cause many habitués of such places to go to the bawdy house district, where they can secure intoxicants and mingle with depraved women."[16]

Laura Bell's departure was only lightly mentioned in March, when the *Iris* reported that "two bawdy houses on Washington have closed during the past week, leaving the number at seven, as it had been until recently. One of the gangs went to Cripple Creek."[17] Laura Bell opened her Cripple Creek bordello at 310 East Myers Avenue, not far from the city's fanciest parlor house, the Old Homestead. In the meantime, Laura Bell's niece, Annie "Little Laura" Horton, moved to Colorado City. Little Laura was born in 1889, to Laura Bell's brother James, in Missouri. By 1906 she was living in Annie Kistler's house, working as a telephone operator.

Laura Bell, meanwhile, was actually working toward returning to Colorado City by constructing an all-new parlor house—a process which perhaps began as early as 1905. The house was complete by

1907, when Laura Bell was back at the new Trilby at 611 Washington Avenue. Directly across the alley was Jacob Schmidt's Place at 612 Colorado Avenue. Now, an underground tunnel connected Schmidt's Place to Laura Bell's. Men could enter the saloon, duck through the tunnel, and enter the Trilby without being seen. Also in town was Laura Bell's old friend, Dusty McCarty, working as a bartender.

In January of 1908 a respectable young man named Tucker Holland committed suicide at the brothel of Dolly Worling. The city council had already been gunning for the red-light district and immediately instructed the police "to at once close all houses of ill-fame and arrest the inmates thereof."[18] This may be the reason Laura Bell appears in 1908 directories as the only resident of the Trilby. She had good cause to worry, because the *Colorado Springs Gazette* noted just a few days after Holland's death that with the cleanup of Colorado City came talk of annexation to Colorado Springs. A February article in the *Iris* claimed that the "exodus of the occupants [of Washington Avenue resorts] is said to be complete and final, and *The Iris* hopes this is and will remain true."[19]

It did not. By January 1909 the girls were back. Just days after Colorado City's mayor notified the women they had ten days to leave town, a series of fires destroyed the red-light district. The largest fire began with a smaller one on January 8, at 11:00 p.m., at the Red Light, a resort located near Seventh Street. That fire was quickly put out, but the next morning at 4:00 a.m., a second fire started in the same building and spread quickly. Fire departments from Colorado City and Colorado Springs, as well as a dozen Colorado Springs policemen, fought in vain to extinguish the flames as high winds hampered their efforts. The flames were so high, they could be seen for miles around and blazed all night.

In the end, nine brothels burned to the ground, including Laura Bell's. The madam moved back to the old Trilby on Grand. The city council was still discussing whether the houses should be allowed to rebuild when Laura Bell and others began making plans to do so—with or without the council's blessing. An April editorial by the *Iris* expressed the paper's discontent: "But lo and behold, no sooner had the new officers held up the hands and taken the oath of office to support the laws of the land, than Laura Bell, the oldest and most influential sinner of them all, started a brick building said to cost $10,000."[20] Construction on Laura Bell's new parlor house, christened "The Mansions," began in May. As the building rose from the ashes, the *Iris* kept up its tirade. "It is hardly probably that the former owner, Laura Bell, would erect a building on the old site except for the old purposes," the newspaper sneered.[21]

The Mansions proved much fancier than the Trilby, with a ballroom, fine furniture, and even livery servants. Upstairs, bedrooms were accessed via a long hallway running the length of the house. The Mansions was indeed palatial, earning Laura Bell the title "Queen of the Colorado City Tenderloin." Old-timers later recalled seeing the madam and her girls as they shopped on Colorado Avenue, wearing fine dresses and acting very ladylike. When Laura Bell, her fellow madams, and nineteen prostitutes were called to court in late May, they were represented by attorneys S. H. Kinsley and W. D. Lombard, as well as city attorney John Watt. Judge Owen warned the defendants that if he saw them in court again, he would send them to jail. The madams each paid fines of $500 for themselves, plus $100 for each of their girls.[22]

But the ladies must have paid hush money to the police as well. In July, when "Alderman Kelly" received several anonymous letters bashing the red-light district, the man merely shrugged his shoulders. "So far as I am personally concerned, I am unaware of the existence of such [red-light district] at the present writing," he told the *Iris*. "I naturally presumed that the fire of last December [*sic*] had forever wiped from existence this so-called 'Necessary Evil.'" Kelly also wrongfully claimed that "the police court of this city has at no time in the past eighteen months, or possibly two years, assessed a fine upon the fallen women." He also added, "I, like Senator John B. Stephen, believe that, if we are to be cursed with this evil, the best way is to confine it to certain quarters of the community, and there control it." He did conclude, however, that "I am not now, nor have I ever at any time, been in favor of licensing the demi-monde."[23]

The fines continued, with Laura Bell paying a total of $365 between July and November. It also was discovered that Dusty McCarty and his wife, Nellie, who now ran the Brunswick saloon on Colorado Avenue, were renting rooms to prostitutes there. The end of the year was capped by the tragic death of retired madam Blanche Burton on December 21, 1909. Heralded as the first official madam of Cripple Creek, Blanche now lived on Colorado Avenue. The night before her death, she was found in the middle of the street after a portiere caught fire and subsequently caught her dress on fire too. She died the next morning.

In January 1910 it was discovered that no fines had been paid by the red-light ladies during the previous December, but Alderman Kelly simply explained he had heard a rumor there would be no fines for that month. As usual, the *Iris* created an uproar, accusing the city of "taking tribute for allowing an immoral cesspool to exist and thrive in its midst."[24] After local ministers took their own vow to help "to eradicate certain notorious resorts where this vice is known to be fostered in Colorado City," Judge Owen finally acquiesced that it "was an open question as to whether the majority of the Colorado City residents wanted the houses closed." After all, the city made lots of money from the ladies' fines and monthly fees. The judge did, however, again warn prostitutes would receive jail time in addition to their fines, "until the law is enforced by the closing of their houses."[25]

In 1910 Little Laura joined her aunt and five prostitutes at the Mansions. Some historians have surmised she was there to learn the prostitution trade. In July, however, Little Laura married Robert Pearson, a barber by trade who resided with the McCartys at the Brunswick House. Laura Bell, meanwhile, may have found an answer to city hall's constant threats. In February 1911 she married Herbert Berg, financial editor of the *Gazette Telegraph* in Colorado Springs, perhaps to gain more power within her realm. When Mayor P. J. Hamble notified the red-light ladies that they had ten days to leave town in April, a news article noted that some had left, but others refused to leave. Laura Bell may very well have been one of them.

For a time, at least, Laura Bell's family and financial circle was safe. The 1912 city directory shows her providing "furnished rooms." Interestingly, Constable Frank Parker was her only boarder, and no other women are listed as living with her. Little else is known of her activities, except that she and Birdie traveled to Denver to witness the marriage of Eva Pearl to Charles Kitto. Herbert Berg, meanwhile, soon tired of his new wife pushing her power around. In 1912 he filed for divorce, which was granted in October. Accordingly, Laura Bell was back in business by 1913, when she and prostitute Jennie Johnson paid another fine in August. But even bigger changes were coming as Colorado City concentrated more than ever on closing down their bawdy houses.

In answer, the saloon men of Colorado City came up with the unique idea to simply create their own town. In May the *Iris* reported that several people were "submitting petitions" to annex the new town, Ramona, which the paper called "Beeropolis."[26] Within a week, forces were lining up in an attempt to keep Ramona dry. A battle over several months ended with a small, inconspicuous note on a back page of the *Iris*: "The election held yesterday in the Ramona townsite to determine whether the residents wished to incorporate was a one-sided affair, as was well known it would be, thirty seven votes being cast for incorporating and none against it."[27]

Laura Bell voiced her opinion on the matter by purchasing property at today's 310 North 24th Street, directly across from Ramona. She continued paying her fines. And when Colorado became one of the first states to enact its own Prohibition law in 1916, she watched as her old saloon friends slowly drifted off or left town. The Mansions, however, continued operating as it always had, and would, if Laura Bell had anything to do with it. After Herbert Berg died, she appeared as "Laura McDaniel," widow, in the city directory. But a second listing showed "Laura Bell" still offered "furnished rooms" at the Mansions address.

With Colorado's Prohibition in place, the Colorado Springs city council drew up a successful plan to annex Colorado City to Colorado Springs in April 1917. Now Laura Bell appeared in the city directory as the widow of Thomas McDaniel. Care of the Mansions is evident by a receipt from plumber Frank Priess, who worked at the house during the fall of 1917. Shortly afterward, on November 20, police showed up at Laura Bell's door with a search warrant. Twenty-seven high-grade bottles of liquor, allegedly stolen from a residence in the elite Broadmoor neighborhood in Colorado Springs, were found. Laura Bell was arrested for "receiving stolen goods," and her trial was set for January 18, 1918.[28]

Witnesses against Laura Bell included Charles Baldwin, the man from whose home the liquor was reportedly stolen. Baldwin was fortunate to have married into money; his wife, Virginia Hobart, was a millionaire heiress to the Comstock Lode in Nevada. In 1907 the couple built Claremont, a beautifully gaudy mansion costing $200,000. The paperwork regarding Laura Bell's final trial on January 24, however, noted that Baldwin was "Out of town. Won't be back soon."[29]

Enter Dusty McCarty, Laura Bell's old friend. McCarty had been blind for several years after suffering a hemorrhage. His wife had left him, and he now worked for Laura Bell while living in the old Trilby on Grand. When he was called as a witness in the trial, McCarty must have shocked everyone when he testified that two men had stolen the liquor from Baldwin's home and deliberately planted it at Laura Bell's.

The madam was found "not guilty," and her case was dismissed at the request of counsel.[30]

Victorious, Laura Bell, Little Laura, and McCarty left for Denver the very next day. The ladies were taking McCarty "to see an imminent eye surgeon."[31] Little Laura now lived in Denver, working a respectable job at a telegraph company, and it was she who jumped behind the wheel of her aunt's Mitchell touring car. The merry group drove north for about forty miles. At a point just south of Castle Rock, however, the car inexplicably rolled as it sped down the highway. McCarty was thrown clear and knocked unconscious. Little Laura fared much worse, her head becoming caught under one of the wheels. She died within minutes. Laura Bell was found under the car, also unconscious, with "seven or eight ribs that punctured her lungs."[32]

The victims were taken to the nearest hotel, and Douglas County coroner Charles Anderson arranged to have Little Laura's body sent to Colorado Springs. McCarty regained "partial consciousness" and also was taken to Colorado Springs. Laura Bell was transported to Colorado Springs on a Denver and Rio Grande train, the fastest method of transportation at the time.[33] She died that evening. Coroner D. Flaw summoned Birdie and Harry Hooyer from Cripple Creek.

Newspapers turned their attentions to the accident itself. Little Laura was driving between thirty and forty miles per hour prior to the crash, an amazing speed for 1918. "The accident seems to be the result of fast driving," concluded Castle Rock's *Record-Journal*.[34] But nobody seemed to question why the only witnesses to the accident were Colorado Springs deputy district attorney Jack Carruthers and two other men identified as Carl Blackman and George Curtis. Carruthers merely said that as they watched (from a point two hundred yards *ahead* of Laura Bell's car), "suddenly it seemed to wabble and then turned over three times, alighting on its wheels, almost in the center of the road."[35]

The men said that they immediately stopped "and went to the assistance of the women."[36]

Were Carruthers and his bunch trying to scare Laura Bell by chasing her car down a lonely highway and zooming past just as it crashed? Or was this a very real, and successful, attempt to do away with a madam who had been throwing her weight around Colorado City for decades? Alas, there was no other investigation into the accident. The case was closed.

Eva Pearl was summoned from Casper, Wyoming. She, along with the Hooyers, oversaw the elaborate funeral and burial of Laura Bell and Little Laura at Fairview Cemetery. Laura Bell left no will, but her estate consisted of over $26,000 in cash, jewelry, property, and other assets. Following the estate settlement, Eva Pearl received everything. Laura Bell's family had her grave moved to a plot at the front entrance of Fairview Cemetery in 1921. Whether it was simply to keep ghouls from disturbing her grave is unknown, but today, everyone entering the graveyard cannot help but pass by Colorado City's Queen of the Tenderloin.

PEARL DEVERE

The Pearl of Cripple Creek

"The Girl Who Could Never Go Home"
This is the tale of a different house-
"The Homestead" was its name-
Which brought a famous mining town
A different kind of fame.
And those who lived at the Homestead?
Well, they were different too.
For they were the girls who couldn't go home,
The way most girls can do.
They just stayed on at the Homestead,
And each in her special way,
Played at the game of living
And flung her life away.
They say that the gayest of them all
Was a girl called Pearl DeVere,
Who had masked her shame with a trumped-up name
And a gaudy, bright veneer.[1]

The Cripple Creek District, known in its heyday as "The World's Greatest Gold Camp," owes its significance to a large and deep volcano measuring roughly twenty-four square miles. Millions of years ago the volcano collapsed, creating giant cracks and fissures into which molten lava flowed. The lava was rich in minerals, including lots of gold, which cooled and hardened over time. It was cowboy Bob Womack, whose family established a cattle ranch in the area during the 1870s, who first discovered the gold. But it wasn't until about 1891 that he was able to convince others of the rich deposits the Cripple Creek District had to offer. Within a few short years, dozens of men would become millionaires as hundreds of others became incredibly wealthy.

Womack's achievement led to the eventual building of over twenty-five towns and camps in the Cripple Creek mining district. The largest of these was Cripple Creek, which aspired to be a first-class city for the rich. By 1893 the city was in a constant state of progress, with new construction, new stage roads, telephone and telegraph lines, and even electricity. The growing population naturally included dozens of soiled doves, who eventually settled on East Myers Avenue, one block south of the downtown area on Bennett Avenue. In time, class and ethnicity divided the neighborhood, with fancy parlor houses, French houses, and lower-class cribs staking their separate pieces of ground. The poorest prostitutes worked in Poverty Gulch on the very east end of Myers, just outside the city limits.

Smaller towns around Cripple Creek, including Altman, Barry, and Victor, also were home to handfuls of prostitutes. At Altman in 1893 the denizens of the red-light district staged a walkout from the fledgling town, along with everyone else, during the first of two labor wars to take place in the district. In Victor, the second-largest city in the mining district, three separate red-light districts flourished over time. But it was Cripple Creek where the district's budding millionaires preferred spending their time, and where the best of the best in bawdy entertainment could be had. Working girls with a head for business could make lots of money here and perhaps even marry a rich suitor. Doing so took talent, looks, and charm, and there was a lot of competition. The right madam could glean the wealthiest of customers by offering the best in services in the way of card games, music, wine, food, and, of course, sex.

By far the best-known madam in Cripple Creek today is Pearl DeVere. The lady is most intriguing, largely because her last parlor house, the Old Homestead House, survives as a museum today and is the only remainder of Myers Avenue's bawdy past. But facts about Pearl's beginnings are quite blurry, to the extent that even today no one has been able to find reliable information about her past. Newspapers of the time reported that she was about thirty-six years old at her time of death in 1897; that she came from Evansville, Indiana; and that she was once married to Ed Martin, a name she was known by in Denver when she was "quite wealthy." They also said her "real" name was Mrs. Charles B. Flynn, whom she married in about 1895, and that her brother-in-law's name was J. L. Weil. Another account claimed she once lived with a well-known gambler named Dietz, with whom she traveled the world before the man "blew his brains out after breaking the bank" at Monte Carlo.[2]

The names of Pearl's family members, how she got to Colorado, or why she chose Cripple Creek remain a mystery, although one report on her death claimed both her mother and sister still lived in Evansville. Historians, both professional and amateur, have researched the few known facts about Pearl for decades, running into one dead end after another. In lieu of solid information, a bevy of untrue tales have been generated about the lady to the extent that she is now quite literally the stuff of legend. What is known for sure is that Pearl and her glamorous Old Homestead garnered a reputation that is still talked about, well over a century after her death.

In the Cripple Creek District, Pearl first appears on record in August of 1894 when she, under the name Isabelle Martin, partnered with one Eva Prince to purchase property in the town of Gillett above

Cripple Creek. The new Midland Terminal Railroad was coming to the district, and would reach Gillett first, on Independence Day. The new town attracted such influential men as Albert E. Carlton, Charles Tutt, and Spencer Penrose, who foresaw Gillett as an entertainment mecca. Tutt and Penrose built an exclusive horse track and the Monte Carlo Casino, and called it "Sportsman's Park." They, along with Carlton, would become three of the district's wealthiest millionaires. With plans to build a $150,000 fancy railway station with a "resort hotel," Gillett looked like a promising place for prostitution to naturally thrive.[3]

Unfortunately, Tutt and Penrose soon realized that their wealthy friends were quite content patronizing the elite Broadmoor Casino in Colorado Springs, rather than making the trek all the way to Gillett. Thus, the racetrack at Sportsman's Park never opened for more than two days a week and eventually scaled down to just a few Saturdays in the summer. The newly built Monte Carlo Casino suffered the same fate and was eventually converted to a school for the children of the town. Pearl and Eva soon relocated to Cripple Creek, which seemed much more promising, and initially purchased property at 319 Myers Avenue in May 1894.

Pearl and Eva appear to have parted ways by the time Pearl advertised in the *Traveler's Night Guide of Colorado*, a pocket-size directory of pleasure resorts throughout the state circa 1894. "The Curfew will not Ring Tonight," read the advertisement, "But our lunch bell rings at 10:30 every evening. All are cordially invited. Ten attractive entertainers attired in white will wait upon you at Pearl DeVere's, 329 Myers Avenue."[4] Within a year Pearl had moved next door to 327 Myers Avenue, on the same lot on which the Old Homestead would later appear. Eva Prince, meanwhile, relocated to 321–323 Myers Avenue, at what was known as the Mikado. Cripple Creek's Sanborn map of December 1894 shows the two brothels connected by a common overhead walkway. Four small structures, possibly cribs, occupied the lot in between them.

Although Eva's building was larger, both she and Pearl featured two-story bordellos with enough room to entertain plenty of customers. The lot the women had originally purchased adjoined Eva's property, and in July 1895 Pearl sold her half of the property to her partner.

Everyone, it seemed, had a stake in Myers Avenue during 1895. Property owners included women but also several prominent men, including Tutt and Penrose, who owned madam Lola Livingston's parlor house and the Topic Theater. On February 1, 1896, Pearl was able to purchase the property at 327 Myers from investor P. E. C. Burke, with a down payment of $800 and monthly mortgage of $600. Just a month later, prostitute Bessie LeClair "filled up with absinthe, and after breaking half the furniture in the Old Homestead landed in jail. She kept the other prisoners awake all night by her screaming, but the 'molly' turned up in the morning and got her out. Her trial will come up Monday."[5]

Bessie's little outburst was just the beginning of troubles for Pearl and the other ladies of the demimonde. In April the first of two fires within a week started on the second floor of the Central Dance Hall on Myers Avenue. The entire red-light district, along with a good portion of businesses on Bennett Avenue, burned. As Cripple Creek rebuilt, the *Colorado Springs Gazette* noted that "entertainment and dance halls, grog shops and nameless places of vice are down below the business level [Bennett Avenue]. Myers Avenue is still given over to buildings of questionable purpose."[6]

Like everyone else on Myers Avenue, Pearl started over. In July she was able to secure a loan from investor Charles E. Howard to rebuild. Pearl would call her new parlor house the Old Homestead, and she intended it to be the most palatial house of pleasure Cripple Creek had ever seen. And it was! The bottom floor included two parlors, an "ante" room for playing poker, and a "drawing, or ball room." Off of the ballroom were a kitchen and a small wine room. Upstairs were five bedrooms, as well as a bathroom with a tub. There was one other interesting feature on the second floor: The bathroom adjoined an upstairs closet with a glass door. Pearl's employees could disrobe and step into the closet, allowing customers to view them without touching them. The walls throughout the house were adorned with fancy wallpaper, lace curtains covered the windows, and Moquette carpets were spread on the floors. Electric lights, running water, and a telephone assured maximum comfort for both residents and visitors. Pearl's private room was off the dining room, allowing her privacy from the rest of the house.[7]

Pearl's employees in 1896 included Wellie Boudine, Ella Dickenson, Ida Grey, Flora Hasting, Mable White, Mayme Wellington, Lola Livingston, cook America "Mary" Samuels, and twenty-five-year-old Inda Allen, housekeeper. These and other employees would come and go as Pearl continued building up her business. In December she borrowed two notes totaling $3,100 from an investor, Orinda J. Straile of New York City. Then, in January of 1897, Pearl bought a Kimball upright piano from the Knight-Campbell Music Company on credit and took out a chattel mortgage for over $2,000 worth of new furniture from the Booth Furniture Company.

The new furnishings were distributed throughout the house; each bedroom upstairs now featured its own unique three-piece boudoir set, toiletries, a chair, lace curtains, and ingrain carpet. Downstairs, Pearl's oak bedstead was complemented by a bird's-eye wood wardrobe, a dresser with a beveled mirror, and two rocking chairs. A writing desk provided a place to do the books. A large sofa and a corner table gave the madam a place to conduct business, relax, or entertain. French mirrors and a gilt-frame picture decorated the walls. A small stove and an oak commode completed the room.

Pearl's debts continued to mount. Beginning in August 1896, doctor appointments for Pearl and her girls, including several "night visits," were billed to the madam. Other creditors included the Silver State Liquor Company, liquor dealers Asmussen & Erickson, the

Parisian Cloak and Suit Parlors, and Fairley Brothers Company. Most interesting is a debt Pearl acquired in March of 1897, when she borrowed $183 from one Emma Gill, giving the woman a ring with three diamonds as collateral. Pearl was apparently cash poor and property rich. In addition, she still owed money to Orinda Straile—a debt she had not paid by June.[8]

Certainly Pearl threw yet another of her lavish parties on Saturday, June 4, in anticipation of making more money. The soiree lasted all night. Pearl retired around 7:00 a.m. in the room of one of her girls, Maud Stone. Pearl "declared she was not able to sleep, and in order to induce slumber took a dose of morphine, something unusual for her."[9] Around 11:00 a.m., Maud awoke to the sound of Pearl breathing heavily and could not wake her. Drs. J. A. Hereford and George Kerr were summoned, but Pearl died later that afternoon.[10] One of the legends about Pearl claims she committed suicide, but the *Cripple Creek Times* clarified that "There is no evidence that the act was intentional."[11]

A deputy sheriff "took possession of the house, had all the girls move out and placed a guard over the valuables" as Charles Howard was appointed executor of Pearl's estate and began looking for her relatives.[12] It was known she "left surviving her a husband, who resides . . . in the Republic of Mexico." The man was soon identified as Charles B. Flynn, who in fact owed Pearl money. Flynn declined to return to Colorado and eventually only paid back a portion of his debt to the estate.[13] Next, Pearl's brother-in-law, J. L. Weil, telegraphed to have the body embalmed and sent to her old home in Evansville, Indiana. When the family discovered Pearl's true occupation, however, her sister refused to claim the body.

Pearl was buried in Cripple Creek's Mount Pisgah Cemetery on June 8 at a cost of $210.25, including what was no doubt an ornate casket for $115. Legend states that an anonymous admirer—perhaps the same man who spurned Pearl's love and drove her to suicide—sent much

Pearl DeVere's Old Homestead as it appeared shortly after becoming a museum in 1958.
Courtesy Jan MacKell Collins.

more than the funeral cost for a much more lavish affair, and that he requested Pearl be buried in a thousand-dollar dress he purchased. Legend also states a twenty-piece band from the Elks Lodge, four mounted policemen, and a slew of admirers were in the funeral procession. The legend further claims that afterward, the procession marched back to town to the tune of "There'll Be a Hot Time in the Old Town Tonight." Legend certainly states a lot, and if the story ain't true, it ought to be. Pearl's grave was marked with a simple wooden marker; in about 1953, the Cripple Creek District Museum would pay for the heart-shaped marble headstone visitors see today.

Howard began settling the few debts owed to Pearl, and the many debts she owed to others, conducting an inventory of her property (including the Old Homestead but also her lot in Gillett), selling everything, and closing the estate. Pearl's jewelry, consisting of several gold and diamond rings, earrings, a stickpin, breastpins, and a watch, were deposited for safekeeping with the Colorado Finance and Safe Deposit

Company on Bennett Avenue. The lady may have died in debt, but she had much to show for it. Her total estate, including her properties, furniture, jewelry, and clothing, plus stock in the Victor Gold Mining, Drainage, Transportation and Tunnel Site Company, and the Ela Helean Gold Mining Company, was appraised at over $7,000 in real and personal property.

At an auction on January 8, 1898, five local businessmen—Oscar Lampman, J. F. Hadley, H. A. Clapp, J. G. Raine, and Cohn Brothers—purchased Pearl's personal items. Raine, a jeweler by trade, bought all of her clothing, listed in the estate as:

Item	Value	Amount Pd.
1 sealskin coat	$100	$50.50
1 Persian silk dress	$25	$14.10
1 blue Eaton suit	$10	$5
1 blue silk tea gown	$4	$2
1 crepon wrapper	$4	$2
1 blue serge dress, silk-lined waist	$4	$2
1 black silk striped skirt	$2	$1
1 white silk tea gown	$2	$1
1 bathrobe	$1	$1.50
1 red silk underskirt	$1	$.50
1 striped silk waist	$1	$.50
2 cotton flannel shirts	$.50	$.25
2 linen night shirts	$.50	$.25
1 black moire skirt	$.50	$.25
1 calico wrapper	$.25	$.15
1 black belt & silver buckle	$.50	$.25
1 red striped silk wrapper	$2.50	$1.25[14]

As for the grand Old Homestead, the parlor house was awarded to Orinda Straile. In 1899 the investor sold the house to twenty-three-year-old Hazel Vernon for $5,000. The Old Homestead remained in business for nearly three more decades before being used for a time as a private home. In 1958 Harold and Lodi Hern purchased the house and opened it as a museum, which is now owned by Old Homestead Museum Inc. and remains in operation to this day.

FRENCH BLANCHE

———•◦•———

A Damaged Dove

Today, Cripple Creek madam Pearl DeVere remains the epitome of the elite madams who enjoyed success, wealth, and fame in the prostitution industry. At the other end of the spectrum in the Cripple Creek District was "French Blanche" LaCroix, an immigrant whose life was anything but cheery. Biographies of women like Blanche are seldom complete, but although she left behind few clues about her life, there is enough information to make hers a story very much worth telling.[1]

The enigmatic Blanche was born in Paris, France, on August 3, 1880. In her youth, she was quite beautiful. Blanche told others she was kidnapped and brought to America to work as a prostitute in New Orleans. A saloon owner, identified by Blanche as "Morris Durant," convinced her to come to Cripple Creek. There was no such person by that name in Cripple Creek at the time, but the man in question was no doubt Marius Durand. The saloon owner first appeared in 1905, running a tavern at South Fourth Street and Myers Avenue—the same year Blanche stated she immigrated to America.[2]

Durand was an interesting character. By 1906 he was known as the manager of boxer Freddie Weeks, who fought in a match in Leadville in December. Roughly two years later he was romancing Miss Josephine Emery, a French bawdy-house girl in Cripple Creek some twenty-seven years his junior. In 1910 Durand, who now ran the Diamond Saloon in Victor, married Josephine. Durand may have found Blanche and brought her to Cripple Creek, but she does not appear on record until 1910.

By the time Blanche arrived in Cripple Creek, the city had spent the last decade trying to do away with the red-light district on Myers Avenue. The efforts were limited at best; in 1904 world traveler and author Lowell Thomas, who grew up in Victor, guessed there were still about three hundred prostitutes on Myers Avenue. Notably, the ax-wielding anti-saloonist Carrie Nation visited town in 1906. Eventually a series of ordinances were put into play. One of them limited prostitutes to doing their shopping on Bennett only one day a week. Another prohibited dance-hall girls from raising their skirts no more than six inches above their ankles.

As for Blanche, she was not working as a prostitute in 1910. The census found her living at the home of Harris Chapman on El Paso Street, far from the red-light district, and working as a private cook for a family. Beginning in 1911, when officials began keeping a register of the prostitutes in town, Blanche did not appear on the list. Still, a slew of people—from author Mabel Barbee Lee, who lived in Cripple Creek at the same time as Blanche to others who knew her as an old woman—agree that she did indeed work on Myers Avenue for a time. Even madam Laura Evens of Salida knew about her.

Durand was still around too, as evidenced by his pledge in 1914 to "open in [Cripple Creek] one of the largest wholesale beer and liquor houses in the state."[3] Two years later, when Colorado enacted its own prohibition against liquor, a Sheriff Kingston made an even more concerted effort to rid Cripple Creek of its soiled doves. But some of the girls, under such old nicknames as "N***** Mollie" and "Liverlip," had no money to leave town, and nowhere to go. French Blanche was one of these women.[4]

The most lurid tale about Blanche was that she had an affair with Durand and became pregnant by him. When Josephine Durand found out about the matter, she allegedly threw acid in Blanche's face. What is known for sure is that Blanche's daughter, Katherine, was born in Cripple Creek on December 21, 1918. At the time, Blanche was living at the Idaho rooming house at 103 East Masonic Avenue, within half a block of the red-light district.

Who really was the child's father? He has been identified as William Chuckman, who fails to materialize in any records for the Cripple Creek District, but the child also was given the surname of Wilcock. Another source has identified her by her married name, Katherine Denny. And there is more: By 1920 Blanche and her daughter had moved to the Arlington, a large but rundown rooming house run by one M. Tregonna. This time, the child's name was listed as Dora. Blanche told the census taker for that year that she was a widow and worked as a servant. She also stated she became a United States citizen in 1915, which is unfounded. Over in Victor were the Durands, where Marius now ran a cigar store. The couple left the Cripple Creek District in about 1921 and landed in Goldfield, Nevada, where Marius opened the Mozart Club and continued promoting fights; one of his clients was boxer Jack Dempsey, whose career began in Victor.

Unfortunately, Blanche was not the ideal mother. On May 5, 1922, at 11:00 p.m., "Katherine Wilcock" was taken from the Arlington, along with three other children, by Sheriff Henry Von Phul. The children were noted as "not sick" but were delivered to the Teller County Hospital. Von Phul had also arrested one Bessie Myers in the incident, which was recorded by hospital records but does not give any additional insight. Katherine remained in the care of the hospital staff until she was discharged on May 14.[5]

On October 2, 1923, Katherine was admitted to the hospital again, this time with a case of eczema. She remained a charge at the hospital for nearly three weeks and was discharged on October 22 "by order of the county judge."[6] It is believed that about this time, Katherine was taken away from Blanche by the Teller County court. Local legend claims that Blanche was able to secure the help of attorney Daisy Barbee, the first female attorney in Missouri, whose clients were nearly all prostitutes. Barbee succeeded in winning Blanche's case, but a celebration party that turned into a drunken brawl caused Blanche to lose Katherine for good and the child was given up for adoption.

Blanche's whereabouts are unknown for quite some years, and she does not appear in the 1930 census. Eventually, however, she landed in Midway, a onetime whistle-stop on the Cripple Creek District Interurban Line. At 10,487 feet in altitude, the faded town afforded majestic views of the Cripple Creek District, as well as the Sangre de Cristo mountains some distance away. The last grocery store in town closed in about 1916, and the only other notable business building was McKillip and Doyle's boarded-up Grand View Saloon, which sat across from Blanche's cabin.

Blanche was not alone at Midway. Her neighbors included Robert "Monty" Montgomery, a miner who lived next door. The two dated for a time, until Blanche caught Monty seeing another former working girl named Annie Bowers from the nearby town of Independence. Blanche and Annie stayed friends, but Blanche never spoke to Monty again. Another of her friends was known as Katie Smith. Later, she would also become friends with local resident Ned Blackburn. Few others were able to get close to Blanche. Locals remembered seeing her from a distance, sitting in the afternoon sun from the window of her cabin. To disguise the scars on her face, she also wore a brown veil when out in public for many years. Although she waved at folks passing by her cabin, Blanche never answered her door without her veil in place.

In October 1938 Blackburn brought Blanche to the Teller County Hospital after she fractured her shoulder. Blanche gave only limited information to the hospital staff, although she remained in their care for nearly a month. When she was discharged in November, she returned to Midway. She managed to elude the census taker again in 1940, but plenty of people remembered her living there.

During Blanche's time at Midway, the community was in the throes of becoming a ghost town. There were no businesses, so Blanche walked to the nearest grocery in Victor some distance away for her shopping needs. Lifelong Victor resident Sally McCready Johnson said Blanche would buy her groceries and reserve enough money to have a drink at one of the local taverns before heading back to Midway. Jim Keener, who grew up in the area, remembered "being with my dad on several occasions when he drove down from his office in Winfield to Victor." Keener was four or five years old and, with his father, saw Blanche walking home on several occasions. She was "carrying her meagre purchases . . . She wore clothes that were more like rags than garments. She always had a crudely-knitted scarf over her head and wrapped around her neck."[7]

Keener's father would stop and offer Blanche a ride, which she always accepted, putting her water and food in the back of the truck before climbing into the passenger seat. Young Keener, squeezed into the middle of the seat between Blanche and his father, observed that Blanche "was a fearsome looking old woman to me as a little boy. The skin on her face looked like wax. She had the hooked nose of an eagle. She was dirty and smelled pretty rank. Her clothes, such as they were, were filthy; they hadn't been washed in years." Keener regarded the encounters with Blanche as strange. "She never spoke, either to me or to dad," he recalled. "She rarely looked at anyone and when she did she glared at people with the look of hatred in her eyes. She looked as if she was angry from the depths of her soul. I believe she viewed herself as having been mistreated her whole life, which she probably was."[8] When the Keener truck arrived at Midway, Blanche "never said thanks or made any acknowledgement that Dad or I existed." Even at his young

French Blanche poses with friends outside of her Midway home during the 1950s. The man on the right is writer Bill Lehr.
Courtesy Dianne Hartshorn.

age, Keener could gather that Blanche "lived probably the roughest life of anyone I ever knew or knew of. She was angry and terribly unhappy about her wasted life as a prostitute."[9]

Steve Mackin, who grew up in Cripple Creek, also was just a boy when he heard of French Blanche. "She kind of scared people," he said. Still, as he rambled around the mostly abandoned district with his friends, Mackin would occasionally dare to call on Blanche. In contrast to Keener's observations, the boys found Blanche quite friendly. "She made the most incredible cookies," Mackin recalled. He noted that her tiny cabin was wallpapered over heavy cardboard under a whitewashed ceiling. The cabin seemed clean enough to him, and featured a green and white porcelain cookstove. Old dynamite boxes were used as shelves.[10]

After a time, Victor resident Edna McCready began taking groceries to Blanche and eventually offered her a home in town. The house was near the McCreadys' house, and Edna took care of Blanche. She also talked Victor city officials into giving Blanche thirty-five dollars per month because she wasn't a US citizen and had nothing to live on. Edna's daughter, Sally, remembered Blanche as being "nice, and quiet." When Sally married and had her own daughter, Blanche gave the child a baby doll.[11] "I remember Blanche," recalled Sally's daughter, Paula Johnson Waddington. "I saw her a few times outside talking to Grandma, but Grandma always shooed me away if I was getting to close. Maybe Blanche didn't want a little kid around to make her think of her daughter." Like Jim Keener, Waddington also described Blanche as wearing "a dress and an apron and a scarf on her head."[12]

In November of 1959, Blanche contracted pneumonia. Her condition worsened, and a neighbor named May Dunn took her to Hilltop Clinic at the old St. Nicholas Hospital in Cripple Creek. Blanche died on November 23. She had told Edna and Sally to look in a certain drawer in her cabin, where the women found $200 stashed away to use for Blanche's burial at Victor's Sunnyside Cemetery. The total cost was $235, which included a casket, minister, and music. Edna bought a small metal address marker on a post to use as Blanche's grave marker.

French Blanche's story doesn't end here. Two years after she died, the daughter she had been forced to give up years ago came looking for her. Accompanying her was her husband. The woman, now in her thirties, said she had been taken by a doctor in Kansas, who revealed her adoption and her mother's true identity on his deathbed. She was given a photograph of Blanche taken when she was about in her twenties, along with a few of her belongings, then disappeared. Today Blanche is remembered by her little cabin from Midway, which the city of Cripple Creek rescued from demolition and donated to the Cripple Creek District Museum in 2010. Today the cabin remains on display and is furnished to illustrate the way Blanche kept it when she lived there.

SPUDS MURPHY

———•••———

"Poor Little Spuddy"

Long after madam Mollie May died in Leadville in 1887, the city's red-light districts remained quite lively, with plenty of other working girls. One of them was Laura Evens, later of Salida, who remained in Leadville during 1895 and 1896. Laura's "best girl friend" was Etta "Spuds" Murphy. "I spent my money as fast I made it," Laura said, "but Spuddy saved most of hers. Sewed $100 bills in her petticoat."[1] Laura later said that Etta would "wait till she got fifty dollars and then she would get a fifty dollar bill. She even had thousand dollar bills sewed up in her petticoats." In Leadville, Laura sometimes called Etta "Brady," possibly her maiden or married name.[2]

The spunky Laura also remembered occasionally getting into trouble with Etta. One night in 1896, the twosome drove a sleigh right into the Leadville Ice Palace. The Palace was a grand undertaking, built entirely of ice blocks as a tourist attraction. When finished, the structure measured 435 feet in length and featured ballrooms, bands, exhibits with "handsome displays" that included a working locomotive, and a skating rink. In many areas, flowers, exotic fruits, taxidermied animals, and even kegs of beer were frozen into the walls.[3] Into this amazing exhibition sailed Laura and Etta in a small cart, but the fun didn't last long. Their horse "got scared at the music and kicked the hell out of our sleigh and broke the shafts and ran away and kicked one of the 4 × 4' ice pillars all to pieces and ruined the exhibits before he ran home to his stable." Another time, Laura and Etta attended a masquerade ball at the Ice Palace.[4]

Indeed, Laura loved practical jokes and acting the scamp, and Etta willingly went along with her. But when Leadville authorities chased many of the red-light ladies out of town in 1896, the women went their separate ways. Laura went to Salida, while Etta departed for Pueblo.[5] Even so, Laura kept track of Etta and told a most interesting story of just how her friend got to Pueblo. "Brady was taken to Pueblo, kidnapped down there and kept," she said. "We hadn't only seven thousand dollars between us when we came down from Leadville . . . so this friend of hers gave her five hundred dollars to come to Pueblo and stay a week. He was crazy, and his family put him out in Werk's sanitarium, took her and put her out in a shanty and an old n***** to watch her."[6] Etta, according to Laura, managed to use her diamond ring to cut a hole in the window and dropped a dollar out. "Some kids come out there playin'—she'd been there for six weeks—and sent me a wire," Laura said. "Well, I went right down and I got her. She wouldn't come up to Salida." A man by the name of Spuddy Murphy was a big gambler in Pueblo at the time, Laura said, and "they called [Etta] Spuddy, like him."[7]

Etta proved quite elusive for the next several years, making it difficult to know exactly when she permanently settled in Pueblo. Her first brothel was believed to have been at the corner of First and Summit Streets. Sanborn maps for 1904 show a large two-story building at the corner with two bay windows on the front. She first appears in Pueblo's city directory at 104 Summit Street in 1906. Two years later Etta's brothel was commonly referred to as "Murphy's Resort" and was quite popular. "Everybody that's ever been to Pueblo knows about Spuds Murphy's house," said Laura Evens. That summer, Pueblo authorities cracked down on the saloons and brothels in town by limiting them to segregated districts. Murphy's Resort was accordingly denied a liquor license because the saloon portion of the business was "outside of the saloon district." Etta was undaunted, and by 1910 her brothel was the largest in town. It was quite an achievement, perhaps helped by Pueblo senator David M. Campbell's "prostitution bill," which passed in April of 1909 and targeted only male pimps.[8]

Around this time, according to Laura, Etta had a brother named Johnny in Kansas City and sent him money for college. Nothing else is known about Johnny, including his age or where he and Etta lived in their youth. Certainly Johnny disapproved of what his sister did for a living. "She went back to his graduation and do you know, he refused to acknowledge her," Laura said, "'Cause he knew she was running a house. That woman sent that boy many a hundred dollars."[9]

Unfortunately for Etta, the authorities kicked off the new year by carrying out a secret plan to raid the red-light district. Every prostitute in town was arrested except one unnamed woman, who managed to escape. Fifty-two women were arrested in all, as well as four men found at Etta's place. Four days after the arrests, a local newspaper article revealed how inhumanely the women had been treated during their two-day incarceration. Undersheriff Warren W. Hill had "used unnecessarily insulting language to the women when they were being arrested," the paper charged. Furthermore, the ladies were divided into two rooms, but only a total of five cots and half a dozen blankets were given to them. The heat was turned off at midnight the first night. The inhospitable environment was duly noted by visiting county commissioners, who immediately ordered more cots at a cost of $250. Still, the women complained that what little food they received consisted of some nasty coffee in a bucket and a breakfast of oatmeal with boiled meat. Some of the ladies had asked if they could send out for food and were refused. In the end, the women were released, most with fines.[10]

SPUDS MURPHY

For her part, Etta paid a fine of fifty dollars, but city officials continued to harass her. In 1910 thirty-year-old Charles W. Jackson was noted
as running the "Murphy Resort" saloon. When he tried to renew his
liquor license, he was denied. Certainly, however, Murphy's Resort had
regained its liquor license by February 6 when, according to the *Pueblo
Chieftain*, Police Chief C. C. Sullivan was at Murphy's when he got into
a fight with a local barber and "fired at him a fusillade of shots." Subsequent news items would accuse Sullivan and three other detectives,
C. F. Dellaquadri, John Miller, and Samuel Schurtz, of frolicking with
the ladies before the fight broke out.[11]

Sullivan vehemently defended himself to the police force, explaining, "I had been up all the previous night. I missed my meals on
Thursday. Thursday night I was on my way home, dead tired after
being up 48 hours, when I got word to look for two men wanted for a
serious crime who were supposed to be somewhere around the underworld section . . . We were on police duty. That is all there was to it.
There were no orgies or dances or liquor." A series of investigations
were conducted, during which Etta and others testified the officers
had shown up around midnight and drank five or six rounds of beer.
The fracas occurred, according to Etta, after she threw someone out
and they in turn threw a rock through her window. The officers had
chased after the culprit and Detective Miller fired shots in the air, but
they were unable to catch the perpetrator.[12]

And there was more: After filling their cups, the drunken officers
Miller, Schurtz, and Sullivan had staggered over to another brothel, the
Quinn House, and continued drinking. They even summoned paddy
wagon driver Guy Park to join them. The men wound up in the bedroom of Sarah Brown, who said that Schurtz "almost tore her kimono
off, which was all she had on." Dellaquadri, meanwhile, slept it off at
Etta Murphy's place. In the end, authorities ended with the conclusion

that the "officers were guilty of conduct unbecoming officers of the law." Some of the men were discharged or demoted; Sullivan was simply "no longer allowed to participate in investigations."[13]

Later that same month, when prostitute Marie Noll was arrested and sentenced to jail, it was noted that Etta Murphy "was also functioning outside of the sequestered section" but had not been arrested. Officers responded that "we were not told to arrest the Murphy woman or any of the others, just the Noll woman." Indeed, Etta exercised some sort of power over the entire red-light district, as noted by newspapers in April. At the grand jury trial of brothel operator Pete Froney, it was noted that "Froney seems to be the King of this district, and one Etta Murphy, as representative of several other parties, seems to be the individual who has unlimited power in the management of a portion of the district." Etta even had a business manager, a man named George Ferris, who managed her brothel. This time, authorities pressed the issue further: Chief Sullivan was accused of letting the red-light district continue operating and was finally fired in May.[14]

Etta was back on top by April when the census was taken, an important note since it is apparently the only census record in which she ever appears. She verified that she was born in 1872 in Missouri to Irish immigrants and that she had been married for twenty-one years. Now, she rented a brothel at 127 South Santa Fe Street. Working for her were eight women: Della Newman, Gertrude McDonald, Mona Stacy, Margaret Bradly, Audrey Martin, Lee Hunter, Bessie Davis, and Mary Catlin. The ladies were all between twenty and twenty-four years old. Etta was thirty-eight—too old to work as a prostitute, too young to retire. For the moment, Etta continued to reign supreme in Pueblo's red-light district. In October, however, she was accused of attempting to bribe Pueblo's acting mayor, Dr. H. G. DeTienne, with one hundred dollars. Etta testified that she "merely offered him the money 'in recognition of past services.'" She was fined fifty dollars.[15]

Etta remained in place until January of 1912, when her brothel was raided yet again. As usual, officers found beer being served. Etta's two employees were entertaining men in their rooms while six more men waited in the parlor. The madam had only recently been in court, where she was found not guilty of running a "disorderly house." Etta's attorney, a Mr. Hoffmire, pleaded guilty on her behalf but told the court that Etta's brothel constituted her home and "that it was the first time she had been engaged in that sort of thing for some time." Hoffmire "pleaded for a minimum fine in the case," but Etta paid another fifty-dollar fine while her girls, Blanche Warner and Hazel Hamilton, paid ten dollars each.[16]

Possibly around this time, according to Laura Evens, Etta had "got in with a detective" in Pueblo. She paid for his daughters' educations and even bought them a baby grand piano and dresses as graduation presents. In the end, "she got tired of him. And sought a younger boy, and, went to City Hall . . .[the detective] closed her up . . . wasn't that dirty?"[17] The last raid staged on Etta's place occurred in March 1912. Two women and eight men were arrested. Etta again pleaded guilty and received a fine, but Police Magistrate Crossman "suspended half the fine on the promise that Murphy 'refrain from further operations along this line.'" Etta told the court she was actually trying to sell her brothel to "get away from the district." She also said she had been closed for two nights, but that two female friends were visiting her when a crowd of drunken men showed up and forced their way into her house.[18]

Laura Evens later stated that heavy drinking contributed to Etta's downfall. Her plea to the court almost sounds as if Etta was indeed aware she had a problem and was trying to rectify the situation. She did make good on her efforts to leave the red-light district and moved into the Grand Hotel, a beautiful four-story building that had just recently been added onto and remodeled. The winter of 1912 was particularly harsh, so Etta directed her brothel's female piano player to utilize her former resort as a boardinghouse for unemployed and transient men. All was not what it seemed, however, for from her suite at the Grand, Etta kept a lookout for men needing female company and made arrangements for them as needed.[19]

Eventually, Etta left Pueblo and wound up in Casper, Wyoming's seedy Sand Bar District. Casper was experiencing a huge oil production boom, and men were flocking in by the thousands. In the Sand Bar District, they could find saloons, pool halls, and bawdy houses galore.[20] But Etta was too old, and perhaps too tired, and especially too poor, to start again. Laura Evens heard about Etta's situation and went to Casper to see her. She discovered that her old friend "was doing washing and ironing and cleaning up cribs for any and everybody." Laura asked around about Etta, explaining she wanted to offer her friend a home with her in Salida. After a time, a "little girl came over to me here, she says, 'Spuddy, wouldn't see you.' She says she is an awful drunkard."[21] In another interview, Laura surmised that Etta "was ashamed and wouldn't even see me. Poor little Spuddy."[22]

Laura Evens was in her nineties when she gave a series of interviews to her attorney, Fred Mazzulla, and others. Understandably, her dates were a bit blurry, making it difficult to know when she last saw Etta Murphy. She was quite possibly talking about the end of Etta's life in 1929 when she said, "Well she got pneumonia. In her old cabin there was a little rent [tear] in the carpet." An unnamed man "come in to sympathize with her, tripped on that, fell over on the bed and knocked the breath out of her. He was drunk."[23]

LAURA EVENS

---•◦•---

"Eat, Drink, Go to Bed or Get Out"

By the time the railway town of Salida was founded in 1880, many of its surrounding communities were much experienced in the skin trade. When the first passenger train pulled into town in May, a generous handful of shady ladies were already waiting for male riders to disembark. The ladies initially took up quarters near the railroad tracks, and the houses of ill fame extended into the residential area within a short time. Respectable women of the town were not very comfortable with this arrangement, even if they couldn't always tell who was a prostitute and who wasn't.

The bad girls of Salida soon made themselves known in the way of drug overdoses, public drunkenness, and fighting. When the wild and woolly Lady Gay Dance Hall on Front Street was reported to be closing, it was noted that some of the gals there showed their bare wares in public, often during daylight hours. The Lady Gay did not close, however, and Salida citizens continued putting up with the antics of the inmates.

Not until 1883 did authorities decide to initiate monthly fines and relegate prostitution to an area on Front Street (known today as Sackett Avenue). The ladies had already been warned at least once by Marshal Stingley that they were "getting entirely too loud in their conduct, and that they will have to go slow or skip." Although the women likely settled down for a while after such warnings, new city ordinances also guaranteed that the revelry would break out less often. By July the ordinances were in place and the city was taking in over a hundred dollars in fines per month. Unlike many towns where corrupt police officers quietly upped the fines and kept some of the money for themselves, Salida's town council made sure their officers played it straight. Those who didn't turn in enough money, or were discovered to be doubling fines and taking a cut, were duly dismissed.[1]

In spite of the ordinances, Salida's red-light ladies did sometimes spiral out of control during those early years. But when Laura Evens arrived in 1896, the lady began setting things right in Salida's red-light district.[2] "Miss Laura," as they called her, remained well known and very well liked for nearly sixty years. Laura's no-nonsense approach to the prostitution industry, and life in general, was unique: She didn't put up with much, and although she loved everything about the life she lived and her career, Laura seemed to have never forgotten her ultimate goal of making money, and lots of it. But the way she embraced the city of Salida, her many friends and admirers, and even strangers who crossed her path is truly admirable.

On May 1, 1871, Laura Turner was born in Mobile, Alabama. Her father, whose name remains unknown, was president of what Laura called the "Southern State Historical Society."[3] She spent a short time at a seminary before marrying John Cooper Evens Jr. in about 1889. On October 2, 1890, the couple's first child, Lucille, was born in St. Louis, Missouri. Laura was simply not cut out to be a wife and mother, and she knew it. With baby Lucille, she boarded a train west. Laura admitted that "up until she got on the train with Lucille she had never taken care of the baby," according to Fern "Peggy" Pedro, who once worked for Laura. "She had someone to take care of the child and she had never done it . . . said 'I didn't know what to do.' When the baby cried she said 'I didn't know whether to feed it or what.' And she said 'I'm just not for kids, that is all . . . I never cared to be bothered with it.'"[4] In spite of her feelings, Laura did love Lucille—enough to take the baby with her when she left her husband.

Laura's first destination was Denver. John Evens soon tracked her down, taking work as a bookkeeper by 1891 and likely working to reconcile the marriage. Notably, his residence at 1939 Larimer Street was just one block from the red-light district on Market Street. Laura tried living with him for a time, but it didn't work out. Lucille seemed to be an especial problem. "Christ," Laura later said, "I didn't have enough sense to feed her or change her diapers."[5] Likely much to her chagrin, Laura gave birth to a second baby in 1892, a son who apparently did not live. She was soon studying the prostitution profession. "I was pretty young when I first became a sporting woman," she said, "and loved to sing and dance and get drunk and have a good time. I had a lovely contralto voice. God knows it cost my father plenty of money."[6]

Laura had little use for the likes of Mattie Silks and her "fat old ladies home." To Laura, Mattie "was third class."[7] She must have left Lucille with her husband when she departed Denver in 1894, for her next stop was Central City where she rented madam Lou Bunch's former brothel. After about six months, however, she was "ordered out of town."[8] She also tried working in Park City near Fairplay before migrating to Leadville in 1895, where she remained from February until January of 1896. At the time, there were five parlor houses on Fifth Street, each employing eight to ten girls. Less expensive brothels were on State Street. "They didn't associate with State [Street], don't you see," Laura later explained. "West Fifth Street was s'posed to be the high places."[9]

Laura guessed the average prostitute made between seventy-five and one hundred dollars a night. "It was the prettiest sight to go down on State Street," she said. "That's where I learned everything up there. I was green as grass." Laura quickly learned every trick in the book to get men to spend their money on her. "You let a miner go back up the

mountain with any money, they'd think you were crazy . . . I remember
having men throw a fifty in your lap. And maybe you'd get 'em so full
they couldn't see straight. Champagne, beer—you know, there's tricks
in all trades," she said.[10]

Laura's income allowed her to buy the best in dresses. She recalled
paying between $100 and $150 for her gowns at Madame Frank's
Emporium during the year 1895. "We wore heavy black stockings
embroidered with pink roses," she remembered. "No short skirts and
hustling in doorways like the crib girls."[11] Laura's sense of style afforded
her the luxury of serenading millionaires like Winfield Scott Stratton of
Cripple Creek. How Stratton heard of her remains a mystery, but one
day she was notified that she had a package at the post office in Leadville. When she entered, there sat Stratton; the package was from him
and contained a pink satin dress with a Queen Anne collar and puffed
sleeves. "Step in the other room and put it on, Laura," Stratton told her,
"and let's see how you look in it."[12]

Apparently Stratton did not know Laura was a working girl, and
when she reappeared wearing the dress, the millionaire was impressed.
The express man said, "Don't you know her?" Stratton answered,
"No, I never saw her." The express man was to the point, explaining,
"She's one of our Fifth Street girls." Laura remembered that "[Strat-
ton] couldn't believe it, you see. 'My,' he said, 'she looks like a society
broad.'" Sometime later, Stratton visited Laura again at the brothel
where she worked. "After he got through," she recalled, "he says, 'I'd
like to go slumming.'"[13]

Laura chose raucous State Street for the tour. The two visited a
dance hall that employed one hundred girls, fifty working the day shift
and another fifty working the night shift. Afterward, Stratton took her
to the fancy Vendome Hotel. There, the twosome crashed the elevator
into the third-floor landing. "We didn't know how to stop the thing,"
Laura explained. The manager, a Mr. Morris, threatened to arrest them,

but they managed to rent a room. "Oh what a beyoutiful room!" Laura recalled. Even flannel nightshirts were provided, and the next morning Stratton took her with him to visit some mines. Stratton paid her fifty dollars for her time and came to see her again. "You're so ignorant that I just enjoy the company," he told her. Augusta Tabor, ex-wife of silver millionaire Horace Tabor, once commented, "Oh, Laurry, wouldn't she make a wonderful wife for a man?" Laura replied, "Oh good God, no. I just got rid of one!"[14]

Stratton's rude comments, suggesting they go "slumming" and calling Laura "ignorant," was nothing compared to other prominent men that included Leadville mayor Samuel D. Nicholson. "When he was young, he liked the girls," Laura remembered. "And he'd come in, you know, and every new girl, now he had a great habit of pullin' her dress up and bitin' her, right here, on the leg." Biting was apparently a habit among other men, too, for one time a piano player bit Laura. She was singing a parody of a song, and he told her, "Miss Laura, if you don't sing that song right, I won't play it." "O, you don't have to," Laura quipped. "Well, he comes over and he bites me," she later recalled. Laura hit the man in the face, blacking his eye. "I was new, you know," she explained. "I didn't know people."[15]

The men of Leadville may have been crass, but during labor strikes in May of 1896, Laura proved more courageous than they were. Union men were blocking the entrance to the Maid of Erin mine. A man named Nick told Laura, "We've got to get a parcel . . . up to the Maid of Erin." Nick was referring to the payroll and was afraid to deliver the package himself. Laura later recalled, "I said, 'Give me the stuff. I'll take it up.'" The money—made up of thousand, five hundred, and one hundred dollar bills—was produced. "I just toted it in my bustle," Laura explained. "And I had a heavy corduroy riding skirt, you know, a double skirt, a voluminous thing." Laura successfully delivered the payroll, received fifty dollars for her trouble, and "when I came down, didn't I start to celebrate? I was so nervous." The next day, Laura went to Denver to see railroad tycoon David Moffat. "I'm awfully proud to meet the young lady," he said gratefully, and paid her another hundred dollars.[16]

Laura may have swept rich men off their feet, but she also had a mischievous side. One time her friend Charlie Cavender asked her to make a trip with him to Stringtown, a blue-collar neighborhood of Leadville. Cavender wanted Laura to drive "Old Broken-Tail Charlie," a skittish horse that was afraid of boxcars and who only Laura could control. On the way, however, the horse was frightened by a wagon he mistook for a boxcar, turning "the sleigh over just that quick." Laura let go of the reins as Charlie ran off. She and Cavender rounded up four pints of champagne that had been in the wagon before going and finding the horse.[17]

Following the labor strikes, Leadville authorities set about chasing the lewd women out of town. Laura departed with a suitcase of champagne—a parting gift from the city's saloonkeepers. She remembered sharing some of the champagne with the train crew on the way to Salida, using the remaining five bottles to bribe local officers into letting her set up shop. The first documentation of her in Salida comes in the 1900 census, taken on June 15, which shows her living at a legitimate rooming house. John Evens had remarried two years earlier and would remain in Denver until his death at the Woodcroft Sanitarium, a private mental hospital in Pueblo, in 1917. Daughter Lucille had been relinquished to Laura and now lived with David and Sally VanWinkle in Salida. Lucille, said Laura, "was never a daughter to me . . . as soon as I got here I boarded her out."[18]

Laura soon purchased her own parlor house. Her office was in a bedroom on the ground floor, across from a formal parlor where patrons were greeted. The employees' bedrooms were upstairs. Here, Laura could at last shine. Her love for rolling her own cigarettes, throwing wild parties, collecting dolls, and swearing even when she wouldn't allow her employees to do it soon became well known. Her brass checks (sold to customers for use within the brothel as commerce) supposedly read "Eat, Drink, Go to bed or Get out."[19] Laura herself said, "I used to be mean, too. I never let a customer get away while he still had a penny in his pocket. That would have been against our religion."[20]

Laura also refused to be taken advantage of. One time, she knocked a paramour she identified as Arthur through a window for dancing too much with another woman. Of the incident, Laura recalled that "his head got stuck in the plate glass and like to cut his throat." She also willingly admitted, "When Arthur and I got mad at each other we'd fight with knives, and I've got scars where he cut me up. I loved that man."[21] Her physician, Dr. Curfman, once told her, "Laura, you have the inclination of a tiger-woman." But the lady also had a sense of humor. Laura herself said, "The inscription on my garter buckles was 'All hope abandon, ye who enter here.'"[22]

Of her girls, Laura commanded respect, honesty, good manners, and no nonsense. They respectfully called her "Miss Laura" but also "Mother."[23] One of her employees, identified only as "LaVerne," later said that "Miss Laura never wanted us girls to talk loud, and we were always taught to watch our language. We parlor house girls never used four-letter words." Laura also showed her girls how to check their clients for venereal disease.[24] Her good business sense dictated that her employees be fashionable and classy. As a result, her parlor house became quite successful.

Between 1904 and 1906, Laura built or purchased a set of six cribs— small apartments with joining walls—at 130 West Front Street. Clients usually came to the main house to meet the girls, who would then take them across the street to the cribs. One time, Laura looked across the street to see one of her girls, Maxine, "lying on her back, curtains all up, all the bright lights on . . . stripped stark naked . . . well I couldn't put up with that. Because I always tried to run a first class place." Laura managed to get into Maxine's apartment and pull the curtain down, but on another occasion the woman snuck into Laura's ballroom wearing nothing but a sheer *crepe de chine* dress. "Well I said, isn't that awful? I just tapped her on the shoulder—I said, 'Listen Maxine, I don't mind you coming over here and trying to solicit trade . . . but by God you put on some underwear.'" Maxine refused, but a customer named "Buney" took her to his house. Buney's father soon complained to Laura about Maxine's habitual drunkenness. "You got a good ditch down below," Laura snapped. "Why don't you throw her in the ditch?"[25]

In 1907 the city directory noted that Laura could be reached via telephone at the nearby Saddle Rock Restaurant. Over time, she made lasting friends with many of her girls. One of them, Lillian Powers, came to work for her in about 1909. Born in Wisconsin and subjected to a hellish homelife, Lil worked as a laundress until a coworker advised her that working as a prostitute on the side could yield more money. Lil quit doing laundry and worked her way west, spending time in South Dakota before arriving in Denver. From about 1903 to 1907, she ran a brothel called "The Cupola" in Denver.[26]

In about 1907 Lillian moved again, this time to the mining town of Victor in the Cripple Creek District. Four years later she rented a crib in Cripple Creek, but her landlady was Leola "Leo the Lion" Ahrens, an alcoholic Frenchwoman. Leo soon grew jealous of Lil's business profits and ultimately threatened to kill her. Lil fled to Salida and procured a job with Laura. She worked out of Apartment 1 in the cribs under the name "Fay Weston" and eventually managed them under their new name, "Weston Terrace," for a percentage of the profits. Lil worked for Laura for a total of nine years before opening her own place in Florence. Like Laura, Lil stayed in business until the 1950s, and died at a local nursing home in 1960.[27]

Laura also stayed in touch with her daughter. Lucille married in 1912 in Denver, but when she gave birth to her first child in December, she was in Salida. Her family next moved to Pueblo, where they

The beautiful and brassy Laura Evens sits astride her donkey in Salida, circa 1907.
Courtesy History Colorado, #10027285.

remained until John Evens's death in 1917. Lucille would continue to sporadically visit her mother for several more years. Laura, meanwhile, purchased more property in Salida in 1913. "And then," she said, "I just took a great delight in improving, improving . . ."[28]

Independent to a point, Laura had a few other men in her life besides Arthur. One of them was "Speedy O'Daniels." Fern Pedro said that if Laura got mad and left him, he would have bills sticking out of each pocket when she returned. Laura would pluck them out and keep the money for herself. When he was short, however, Speedy would pilfer Laura's cashbox. She initially blamed her janitor and hid in the dark one night waiting for the thief. When Speedy came into the dark room, she "let him have it with a pool cue and turned the lights on and it was Speedy O'Daniels out cold."[29]

In 1914 Salida authorities finally decided to wage a war against the red-light district. "Without noise, ostentation or the usual 'raid' features associated with such movements, the greater number of resorts in Salida's Red Light District were closed last Saturday," the *Salida Record* reported in July. Laura Evens was excepted, however, and her "large 'parlor house' is to remain open several months longer." Authorities obviously trusted Laura to maintain better control over her ladies, even though Mayor I. C. Alexander declared her place was to be closed by April 1 of the following year. But Laura never did close and bought even more property in 1915.[30]

When the deadly influenza epidemic hit in 1918 and the local hospital ran out of beds, Laura closed her house to make a temporary shelter for the sick. Her girls willingly worked as nurses. "So Doctor Curfman called up," Laura recalled. "He says, 'Laura, have you any girls down there can nurse?'" One of her girls, a woman named Jessie, loved nursing and Laura knew it, so she accordingly sent her to work for Curfman until the epidemic passed.[31] One of Jessie's patients was a minister's wife, and the minister was so grateful that he offered her a job as housekeeper and companion to his wife. Jessie modestly declined, saying, "Now that my job is done, I'll be on my way back to Miss Laura's on Front Street."[32]

Laura continued buying property, but was forced to sell much of it during the 1920s. Courthouse documents are riddled with transactions bearing her name during that time, and local rumor states she nearly lost her properties on several occasions. According to Fern, Laura was seeing a surgeon who talked her into selling her place and took her to Denver. There, the man "got her into a crooked card game. And she lost every cent and went back up and started from scratch again."[33] Laura did have her Front Street parlor house, however, where she would remain the rest of her life.

Laura's continuing wealth matched her giving spirit. During the Great Depression hundreds of food baskets were found on the doorsteps of families with children. Coal was mysteriously delivered free of charge, and a church in town received a new roof. Railroad men who were injured on the job would suddenly receive less-strenuous employment offers while they recuperated. One man recalled that shortly after suffering a severe hand injury, he was offered a job selling newspapers in a local store. The pay was unusually high. "I didn't learn until long after Laura died that she paid the storekeeper for my salary for more than a year while I got over my pain and learned to use what was left of my hand," the man later recalled.[34]

Such good deeds were performed anonymously by Miss Laura and her girls. Young boys who ran errands for Laura after school were invited in no further than the kitchen for hot chocolate or a warm meal during cold weather before being paid, usually ten dollars, for their work. Miss Laura would instruct them to take the money home to their mothers, telling them, "You earned the money in honest work for a stranger." Respectable wives who suffered abuse often sought help from Laura, who gave them shelter and refused to let them work for her. "I doubt if anybody will ever know how many people Laura helped," said a Salida politician in later years. "She was an entire Department of Social Services long before there was such a thing."[35]

Fern Pedro went to work for Laura in 1928, and remembered that things were quite lively at her place. "I have seen nights that I never got dressed," she recalled, commenting that the "crib girls used to get a dollar . . . and Laura's girls two dollars . . . and up." Laura would stand at the foot of the stairs "and let one man up and send another down." Fern and the others kept half of their earnings. On one occasion, Fern recalled, a stranger showed up at the door. Laura was in Pueblo, so he and Fern played a slot machine for bit. Because it was raining, Fern invited the man to bring his dog inside. When she made a bed for the animal, the man gave her twenty-five dollars. The gentleman ended up staying for three nights, giving her a check for a thousand dollars. When Laura returned, it was discovered the wealthy man was one of her long lost friends from Denver.[36]

One of Laura's other consorts was Mike O'Leary, a large, well-dressed man with dark hair and blue eyes, whom she met on one of her frequent trips to Denver. Laura wasn't in love with him, and was always trying to get one of her girls to sleep with him so she didn't have to. O'Leary eventually talked Laura into going to California with him and buying a cottage camp. She even hocked her fur for the effort, but finally tired of the man's antics. She was very sick when she returned to Salida, telling her girls, "If he ever comes near the house I will kill him." A Pueblo physician put her on a special diet, but when someone left four cooked ducks at her door one evening, she ate one. "And that night we had to call . . . Doctor Nicoletti [of Pueblo]," said Fern, "but he really fixed her up . . . cured her." Laura eventually gave up on men and satisfied herself with dispensing advice to her girls. "If he doesn't have money," she said, "just leave him alone."[37]

Only four girls worked for Laura in 1930. She was, after all, nearly sixty years old, and began occupying some of her time by playing a card game called "Pam." She had a small dog, too, given to her by Lillian Powers. Laura called him "Little Pimp Powers" or "Mr. Powers." The dog favored lying on the foot of Laura's bed and would growl at anyone who came near. When he died in about 1935, Laura was playing cards in the next room. "And she threw her hand down," Fern remembered, "and said, 'Mr. Powers is dead.' Walked in there, and sure enough he was." Another time, Fern brought home a black cat. When the cat got pregnant, she was given a bed in Laura's room. The next morning, after an all-night card game, "here are the nicest little bunch of kittens right in the middle of Miss Laura's bed you ever saw," Fern said. Laura made Fern help her clean off the bed, but she kept the kittens.[38]

By 1940 Laura was down to just one employee. Two years later, or possibly as late as 1950, the authorities finally closed her down for good—with apologies. Laura turned to renting rooms to railroad men, however, playing poker with them and often taking their money in the game. Most interestingly the closure resulted in an immediate upswing in sex crimes to the extent that authorities asked Laura to reopen. She declined, explaining she had rented her rooms to railroad men who were "all settled in, and she didn't want to evict them."[39]

Laura's last years were spent playing poker and giving interviews, mostly to her attorney, Fred Mazzulla. A local man remembered that when he visited her once, she had "packed most of her things in trunks and was living in one room in the northeast corner of the building."[40] Laura passed away at her home in 1953. Witnesses claimed that on her deathbed, Laura spread her arms wide and called, "Mother, come and take me." She was buried in a lavender casket and her funeral was reported as quite lavish, but only twenty-six people attended the service.[41] Her parlor house has been owned by the Mon-Ark Shrine Club in the decades following her death.

BESSIE RIVERS

———— •••• ————

"The Swellest Woman You Ever Met"

B ack in 1876, one of several river towns was established in southern Colorado along the Animas River. First called Camp Animas,
the name was soon altered to Animas City. By 1880 the growing town
was home to farmers and miners and became a trade center for those
traveling in any direction. When the Denver and Rio Grande Railroad
tracks were constructed nearby, a new town, Durango, was established. Most of the businesses and residents of Animas City moved to
the new town, although the old town retained a small population for
many more decades.

Like so many other places on the Colorado frontier, Durango was
destined to see an influx of bawdy-house women within a relatively
short time. The women did well. Madams paid a monthly tax of
sixteen dollars, their employees each paid six dollars, and crib and
dance-hall girls paid four. But the city was truly smiled upon by the
arrival of Bessie Rivers, who would become a lifelong landmark in
Durango. Bessie was Frankie Stewart when she was born between
1862 and 1865. Her parents, Horace and Hannah Stewart, were Iowa
farmers. Only one other child came of the union, Bessie's older sister,
Cora. By 1870 the family was in Maquoketa, Iowa, where Frankie and
her sister attended school.

Cora married in 1876, and Frankie followed in 1877. Her chosen mate was a farmer named Charles Fergason, and the two were married in Woodbury County, Iowa. One son, Arthur, was born on June 3, 1878. Cora also had a child that year, and it would appear that the sisters were very close. The 1880 census finds both women and their families living in Grant, Iowa, with their respective spouses and children. Frankie remained in Iowa through 1885, but Cora was gone by then. Frankie left soon too, apparently following her sister to Colorado.

While Cora and her family settled in Silverton, Frankie took a different route and left her husband and son behind. Her travels landed her in Durango, where she first worked as a dance-hall girl before expanding further into the prostitution industry. Within a few years Frankie Fergason became Bessie Rivers, madam of Durango. Bessie was good at her job. They say that when the First National Bank in town began letting women open their own bank accounts, the first woman to do so was the bank president's wife. Bessie was the second.

It is hard to say just where Bessie operated her brothel in her formative years. She might have lost everything, and subsequently moved, when Durango suffered a catastrophic fire in 1889. She was likely working among the other prostitutes who operated in the 900 block of Main Avenue beginning in 1890. The first time Bessie appears on record is 1896, when a man named Edmand Hilf "came to his death by one pistol shot from a Colt Army pistol 38 caliber by his own hands." Witnesses at the coroner's inquiry were Bessie, Laura Preston, Lillie Jackson, and James Edwards.[1]

Bessie was certainly running a brothel of her own by about 1898, when John Arrington of New Mexico chanced to visit her place. Although he was only around nine years old at the time, Arrington later called Bessie Rivers "one of the most wonderful women I have ever met." The boy happened to be with a group of freighters who decided to spend time at Bessie's. He remembered that she employed "between thirty and forty nice looking girls," and that her place had a bar and a "smooth dance floor."[2]

A small boy among a bunch of men immediately caught Bessie's eye. "Come here, young man," she demanded, "I want to talk to you! What is your name and where are you from?" Arrington explained who he was and why he was there. "This is really no place for you," Bessie replied. She gave the boy a dollar and directions to a store called Richie's. "Get yourself an ice cream soda and some of the nice candy they have," she instructed. "Then come back and I will talk to you more." Arrington did as he was told, taking his time on the walk back to the brothel. When he arrived, he "found that Bessie had arranged for me to be taken to the San Juan Livery Stable where my bed was waiting for me to crawl into." Arrington also remembered that Bessie's customers felt comfortable leaving their valuables in her large safe, and that she did not "allow her girls to fleece their customers."[3]

By 1900 Bessie's brothel was located at 730 10th Street. The census taker that year listed her as a "Landlady—Sport" and noted she owned her building free and clear. Living at her house were Georgie Smith, Matie Shefler, May Seibel, and Nellie Boynton, all women aged between twenty-three and thirty years old. Sixty-eight-year-old Thomas Hay was there as well, and whether he was a customer is unknown. Bessie, who was thirty-eight years old, showed no signs of slowing down. During 1901 both she and fellow madam Jennie Moss paid periodic fines of $150 apiece. Bessie also was making gobs of money, as evidenced by the theft of $3,000 in diamonds from her in 1904.

The robbery happened on a Saturday night, but Bessie had a hard time convincing officers that it had occurred. "Some of the papers treated it as a joke, an advertising scheme *a la* actress," revealed the *Telluride Daily Journal* on June 14. "However, yesterday officers recovered the precious stones and cleared Bessie of the imputation of being a fakir."[4] The *Aspen Democrat* finally told the whole story. Burt Jameson,

Bessie's "friend," had stolen the diamonds and "had tried to fasten the theft on different young women associates" of the madam. An officer found the gems, as well as a "night key" to Bessie's house "which was recovered by sluicing a vault." Jameson was taken to Denver.[5]

From all known accounts of her, Bessie was as honest as the day was long. She dutifully paid her fines and her business and liquor license fees. Newspapers revealed enough tidbits about her to make her interesting. She had, for instance, a beloved horse in 1906 who she named George. And, she was very interested in photography and produced her own photographs. "Gonner is exhibiting Harry Thomas' and Bessie Rivers' photographs in the same window," blurted the *Durango Democrat* in December 1906. "Now wouldn't that blow a fuse on a street car?"[6] Gonner's was a music and photography shop, and Bessie maintained a good business relationship with Mr. Gonner. She also remained friends with people in her home state of Iowa, as evidenced by a postcard she received in 1907. A poem on the front was most relevant: "Who loves not women wine and song, will be a fool his whole life long."[7]

By now, Bessie was the proprietress of the Horseshoe Saloon, a fancy tavern and restaurant known for its "elegance and opulence" at 969 Main Avenue. The place was quite large, with a "long, elegant, ornate Victorian bar" running down one side of the room. During the day, a nickel beer came with a free lunch. The meals increased in both quality and quantity as each additional nickel beer was purchased. Dinners were served on fine china at candlelit tables. The menu offered five courses; each recommended pairings of rare wines. Entertainment was provided in a theater in the basement. Wealthier clients merited a visit to Bessie's elegantly appointed apartment upstairs. Behind the saloon was the Horseshoe Café. Also in back was a big brick dance hall, run by a manager who remained close to Bessie until the day she died.[8] Durango local Edna Goodman identified the man as a professional gambler named Charles Cooke.

Bessie entertained her male clientele in the evenings at the Horseshoe and did her shopping by day on the streets of Durango. Marguerite Cantrell's father owned Jackson Hardware, and she remembered Bessie well. "She was a big woman, nice looking, always dressed nice," Marguerite recalled, although she had no idea who Bessie was the first time she saw her. When none of the other clerks would wait on the madam, Marguerite's father told her to do so, and to "be nice to her." Afterward, Marguerite's father explained about Bessie. He said that "a lot of people didn't like to have her come in the store or bring her girls in, nor did they like to wait on her." He instructed Marguerite, "Don't you ever be that way." Marguerite obeyed, and every time Bessie came to the store from then on, she asked for the girl to wait on her.[9]

Marguerite also remembered that Bessie drove "one of those old fashioned phaetons," a buggy made so that one could step right into it. "She used to dress her girls up, four beautiful, beautiful girls and parade up and down Main Street," Marguerite said. At the time, Marguerite was too small to understand what the women did for a living, but she "used to watch those girls. They were so lovely, and they had their big hats on, their umbrellas, and one or two of them would be smoking, which you didn't do in those days."[10]

Everybody, it seemed, liked Bessie—to a point. When she canceled her subscription to the *Durango Democrat* in 1908, the newspaper published a long commentary about her. "Bessie is a virgin in the red," the article said in part. "She pays her license like a citizen and hits the susceptible like a hornet—if they have anything to hit." Bessie, the paper illuminated with tongue in cheek, "was an angel child—a mistress of her mother's lips when a babe—the vine that climbed a father's knee when a girl, and a woman who in later years still climbed. She is yet in the flesh, tender, confiding and adored." The writer ended his tribute with the caveat that "the *Democrat* wouldn't make of her memory a shrine or worship flesh, which is not its own. Grief has its luxury and Bessie has to go—so does the subscription."[11]

Bessie really did have to go, as it turned out. In March the *Durango Democrat* announced that the district attorney, a man named Stidger, was zeroing in on the police, who were slacking in their control over Durango's red-light district. Stidger accordingly gave the soiled doves "twenty four hours to secure honorable employment or they must leave the city."[12] In May an advertisement appeared in the *Democrat*: "For sale—The buildings on my lease, house and outhouses, fences, walks, hardwood flooring—all that is on the land. Bessie Rivers."[13]

But Bessie wasn't going far. Rather, she decided to simply relocate to another property. She was initially denied a new business license, but successfully appealed the decision. When she applied for another new license in 1909, three city councilmen voted against her.[14] Newspapers might have been defending her one Christmas when it was commented that "we don't see any church philanthropists busy, no one, but we sure saw one of the 'fallen women' scattering $5 bills. We know who received them, where they went, the beneficiaries needed every dollar that came their way. And Bessie Rivers opened her purse."[15] Bessie was also in the habit of gathering donations as needed from her girls and other brothels, adding to the pile and presenting it to charities in need.[16]

Bessie's new address as of 1910 was at 313 Main, conveniently close to the railroad depot. Four girls worked for her, including Nellie Boynton, who had now been with Bessie for at least a decade. The following year, she was operating on Railroad Avenue at the southeast corner of 10th Street. Notably, Bessie purchased a malt beer license in 1911 at a cost of $150 per year versus $600 per year for a liquor license. More interesting is that even though Bessie denied she had any children living or dead in the census records, her son Arthur came to visit her in Durango. Arthur had most recently lived in Greeley, but for some reason applied for the $600 liquor license in the 900 block, where Bessie owned most of her property. Arthur may have returned to Iowa the following year, when his father died.

Few remembered Arthur's brief visit, but plenty of folks remembered Bessie when historian Duane Smith interviewed them. One of them was Richard Macomb, who grew up in Durango. "She was cute, yeah, she was a pretty woman," he said of Bessie. "She was very good looking in her younger days. She was a rather large woman. She was fairly heavy, and she was fairly tall, I would say about 5'9" tall. She had maybe six or eight girls working for her." Macomb worked at Parson's Drug Store and remembered that Bessie asked the owner to allow her employees to have charge accounts. "We did quite a little of that, charged," Macomb said, "and, by gosh, those people were the best payers you ever seen . . . She saw to it and their word was good." Bessie, he said, "ran a very respectable place. She was in it to make money. They would sell beer for $1 a bottle."[17]

Times were changing, however. With Prohibition looming in Colorado's future, Bessie decided to revert to her legal name, Frankie Fergason. By 1920 she was running a legitimate rooming house at the former Horseshoe Saloon. During that same year, her sister Cora died after some years of suffering from an unknown ailment. While Cora appears in the census records of Colorado as a family woman, her daughter, Florence Livermore, became a stage actress under the name "Vail de Vernon" and once visited her mother in Silverton while on a performance tour in Denver. As for Cora, Georgia Cook remembered Bessie buying her sister books to read when she was laid up. Cora was laid to rest in Durango's Greenmount Cemetery.[18]

In 1925 Bessie purchased a house in old Animas City, which was slowly being absorbed into Durango. The house, at today's 3310 Main Avenue, was a simple square structure with a fenced yard.[19] Georgia Cook remembered Bessie when she lived there, calling her "one of the

Bessie Rivers's lavish Horseshoe Saloon is now a sandwich shop in downtown Durango.
Courtesy Jan MacKell Collins.

sweetest women you ever met in your life. She would do anything for anybody to help them out . . . Bessie was one of the swellest women you ever met . . . She couldn't stand to see anyone go hungry or anything."[20] Durango local Edna Goodman called Bessie "a very high type person, a perfect lady." She also recalled that Charles Cooke, Bessie's old friend, "looked after her just like he was married to her. He took her every day from her building to this house [in Animas City.]"[21]

Bessie remained a landlady into 1930, renting to mostly male boarders. She also remained in the hearts of Durango residents like Deora Powell, who recalled that Bessie "was really good-hearted. They said that if a man needed a meal, she bought it for him." Eventually Bessie moved back to Durango proper, living in the old Horseshoe Saloon. Without much ado, she died in 1937 and was buried next to Cora in Greenmount Cemetery. Surprisingly, she does not appear to have left anything to Arthur, and locals either purchased or took most of her belongings, some of which remain in Durango today.[22] So ended the life of Durango's best-known queen of hearts.

LOU BUNCH

---•●—

Three Hundred Pounds of Pleasure

Each June since about 1974, Central City—one of Colorado's earliest mining towns in Gilpin County—hosts a wild weekend called "Lou Bunch Days." The event is by far Central City's busiest weekend. For three days, the small town is besieged with bed races, parades, live music, food, and hundreds of women dressed up as their favorite floozy. The event honors madam Lou Bunch, the last of her kind to officially operate in town.[1] Seldom, however, do promoters of this most unique event talk much about Lou herself.

Central City's nightlife had already been in place for some time by the time Lou got there. Within a year of its founding in 1859, the town already had at least one brothel. The place was described as "a sort of hurdy-gurdy saloon, built of rough logs and containing the usual primitive accessories of a dance house." A primitive bar offered "Taos Lightening" with card games and "three or four girls educated in the business of passing drinks and bandying coarse epithets with whomsoever pleased to call them out."[2]

Very early on, Gilpin County was quick to impose laws upon businesses offering pleasures of the flesh and other entertainments. In February of 1861, the county passed a law in Section 42 of its revised and adopted laws that stated, "All gambling houses of ill fame or prostitution shall be considered a public nuisance and treated as such." In the Nevada mining district outside of Central City, the laws were even harsher. A resolution was made that found "counternancing or encouraging of low Body [*sic*] Houses Grog shops and gambling Saloons to be degrading to the sway and peace and order and Disgraceful to the name and character of the District." It was resolved that "there shall be no Bawdy Houses Grog shops or Gambling Saloons within the Limits of this District." A fifty-dollar fine was decreed for anyone breaking the law.[3]

Somehow, however, ladies of the evening were free to ply their trade on Central City's Eureka Street. When a Madam Wright was arrested for larceny on Eureka in the mid-1860s, the *Miner's Register* newspaper commented, "It is high time she were routed out from the place she occupies on one of the most public and respectable streets in our city." The *Miner's Register* further suggested that although "such creatures should be permitted to live in a community," they should be punished for "offenses against morality and law" and perhaps move to "some remote locality where their presence will not be so annoying."[4]

Complaints about the brothels on Eureka Street continued through 1866. One anonymous writer boldly pointed out that while the *Central City Register* openly complained about certain brothels, they failed to mention the one operating right across the street from the newspaper office. More complaints followed after such outrageous acts as the murder of a man at the crib of "Moll Green" in 1867, new crops of brothels popping up throughout the city in 1868, and the Shoo Fly Dance Hall, brazenly opening downtown in 1870. When journalist James Thomson visited a Central City bawdy house two years later, he wrote in his diary about seeing three men and women doing the deed in beds right alongside each other, as well as a woman who stripped to her stockings and danced on the bar.[5]

Eventually Central City's naughty girls migrated to Gunnell Hill above town at the end of Pine Street, just a few blocks from St. Mary's

Lou Bunch

Instantaneous Art Portraits,
New Studios
3136 Cottage Grove Avenue,
TELEPHONE 8354.
CHICAGO.

The only known image of Lou Bunch was taken in Chicago.
Courtesy History Colorado, #10038453.

Catholic Church. The red-light district was eventually dubbed "Quality Row," with girls such as May Martin, Jane Gordon, and Della (or Lizzie) Warwick offering services.[6] For the most part, Central City citizens accepted the red-light district in its rightful place up on the hill. The men enjoyed having a place to go, while the women saw it as a necessary evil. "I don't want my boys to go up there," said one woman, "but when I look over the fence and see those strapping boys of my neighbors and then think of my girls, I believe it all right to have a place where they can go."[7] While Gunnell Hill mostly removed Central City's prostitutes from sight, the close proximity of St. Mary's sometimes proved problematic. One time a twelve-year-old girl ventured up Pine Street after the Sunday morning services. The child witnessed a prostitute standing over the front rail of her porch, dangling a silver crucifix. In the yard below was a man on his knees, begging the woman to give it back.[8]

By 1880 the best-known madam in town was Ada Branch, also known as "Big Swede." Ada dressed well and built a nice parlor house. In 1880 the *Rocky Mountain News* reported on a fight on "Big Swede Avenue" in Central City, illustrating that Pine Street had been temporarily renamed in honor of Ada.[9] The madam also boldly rented the Alhambra Theater downtown in 1881. Her advertisement in the *Daily Register Call* stated, "I have taken a lease of the Alhambra Varieties for one year, and will open there on Friday evening, the 13th of May with a grand ball. A cordial invitation is extended to all. Free to all. Ada Branch."[10]

Ada and others like her certainly deserve their place in Central City's bawdy past. The best remembered madam, however, was Lou Bunch. Weighing in at three hundred pounds, Lou's presence in town surely could not be missed. Today her life is an interesting mixture of fact and fiction, filled with guesses and hearsay from historians and writers with a sprinkling of documentation. But while the enigmatic woman left little trace in the way of hard truth, she certainly bears looking into.

Lou was born in Sweden on February 14, 1857. After immigrating to America in 1868, she eventually wound up in the demimonde of Denver. There, she first took a job with madam Mattie Silks, with whom she would maintain a friendship until Mattie's death in 1929. In 1878 Lou married George Bunch. Much like Lou, George also sports a mysterious past. The 1880 census finds him living in Denver and occupied as a gambler. There is mention of him again in 1883, when he accompanied Charlie Stanton and Stanton's girlfriend out on the town. Afterward, the couple got into a fight over money. Stanton pulled the woman's hair, and she came at him with a knife. She managed to slash Charlie's face a few times before Bunch was able to get him downstairs to the saloon, where whiskey was used to disinfect the wounds while stitches were applied to Charlie's cheek. George was no angel either; he "was convicted of assault and battery against Lou at least once and also of stealing from her."[11]

Although she does not appear in the 1885 Colorado census, at least one historian maintains that Lou became a madam on Denver's infamous Holladay Street that year. Five years later she branched out to Central City, where she initially purchased the brothel of May Martin. Her 1892 appearance at 2026 Market Street in Denver's red-light district confirms that Lou probably operated houses in both cities. This may be why both she and George left some unclaimed mail in Denver during 1893.[12]

In Central City, Lou rented her parlor house out to other women at first. When future Salida madam Laura Evens worked in Central City for about six months in the early 1890s, she remembered that Lou already had gray hair when the two met. Lou, she said, had moved into Ada Branch's former brothel. Laura also remembered three or four other houses, along with madams Nel Warwick and Dell Thompson.[13] Lou was going back to Denver, and Laura rented her brothel from her. With Laura were five girls and a piano player who also played on Central City's baseball team. The house, she remembered, had two front doors and was built into rock with "one room in the center between the two front doors." Walking in, she said, "here was benches, no carpets on the floor . . . And then you went in back and there was a dining room." A hallway to one side led to five bedrooms. According to Laura, there had also once been a second story on the building with two "quite good rooms," but "you had to come outside and go down."[14]

Laura did not like the house. Lou, she said, wasn't the best of housekeepers and had let the brothel "run down hill. When it got out of repair she didn't repair it." Laura remembered that "the toilet was that far from the kitchen, all stuffed up. Oh, it was a terrible place to live . . . This [the front] room was haunted." Laura had heard that "there was a barber up there who murdered a man in that house." Although she disliked the haunted room, Laura recalled that "one night I said, I am going in there to sleep . . . It was the only room that had a stove. She didn't have no fire in that place, we had a stove in this little space." Laura was sleeping when she felt like "something had me around the throat." She and her girls "set up in the dining room the rest of the night."[15]

Despite the house's condition, Laura made good money for the first three months. Her income waned when some of the mines around Central City began shutting down. Once, when she couldn't afford the sixty-dollars-a-month rent, Lou told her, "Oh let your cook lay off. I am going to make some of the most delicious soup." The dish was not as good as Laura hoped. "Well Miss Lou smoked," she said. "I said to one of the girls . . . look the snuff is dropping in the soup . . . Can you eat it, I can't. OH God . . ."[16]

In 1899 Lou moved to Central City on a more permanent basis and purchased one of two "remaining parlor houses." There are many stories about her, some true and some perhaps not. She had a fondness, for instance, for baseball and often attended games at the local ball field.[17]

Ever the "whore with a heart of gold," Lou allegedly turned her brothel into a temporary hospital when some sort of epidemic broke out. The stories about her also include being caught in bed with Central City's mayor, after which his wife ran her out of town on a bed.[18]

On the opposite end of this spectrum is the claim that the "residents of [Gunnell Hill] were careful to send married men away. One time a married man followed the girls from the Shoo Fly to [Lou's] house; they sent him home to his wife, telling him their services were 'for the needy, not the greedy.'"[19] Longtime resident Louis Carter perhaps summed up the truth when he wrote, "The *modus operandi* of these houses was that which was common to the operating of 'Parlor Houses' everywhere. The girls were dressed in conventional clothes, properly coiffured and highly perfumed and incensed. They were to conduct themselves with as much decorum as their avocation allowed."[20]

In 1900, Lou and George Bunch allegedly had a child, who died at the age of ten. Record of the baby is scant, but what is known is that by 1900 Lou Bunch was a permanent resident of Central City. The census that year notes that she lived on notorious Pine Street, had become a naturalized citizen, could speak English, could read and write, and owned her house. Interestingly, her occupation was listed as a gold miner, a vocation that was more tongue in cheek than anyone realized. Only two women, Blanche Campbell and Ida Ramsey, worked for her the day the census taker came by. Also in the house was one James M. Ward, who quite possibly was a customer.

The 1906 Denver City Directory shows Lou living on respectable Curtis Street in Denver, but she was back in Central City by the time of the 1910 census. This time, the census recorded her as renting a place on upper Nevada Street, but her business was the same: Prostitutes Lillie and Hazel Washington and May Young worked for her. At the time, Central City was working hard to close its houses of prostitution. Three years later, Lou's old house on Pine Street burned down.

By 1915 Lou was back in Denver for good, living at 1935 Arapahoe Street. Notably, George Bunch was in Denver too but living at a separate address. Lou continued bouncing around at different addresses through 1920, when she was managing the "Franchant Rooming Home" on 19th Street. For the first time, she was listed in the census as a widow.[21] It was around this time that Lou became "quite good friends" with her former madam, Mattie Silks.[22] Some say that she even moved in with Mattie to take care of her until Mattie passed away in 1929, although city directories do not show them living together. By 1930 she had moved to Aurora, where she worked as a maid for one Joseph Smith. She remained working as a maid as late as 1932.

Lou's last home was on Fox Street in Denver when she died on January 19, 1935. She was buried without much ceremony in Denver's Fairmount Cemetery. Not even a tombstone marked her grave until 2011, when the Gilpin Historical Society expressed their unfulfilled desire to give Lou a proper marker. Dean DiLullo, general manager of Fortune Valley Casino in Central City, heard of the cause and arranged for a donation for a lovely tombstone. The stone reads, "a Lady, loved by many."[23]

MAE PHELPS

---•●•---

A High-Toned Hussey

Because Trinidad was located right along the Santa Fe Trail, the city's illicit nightlife is likely to have begun a lot earlier than in most Colorado towns. Permanent settlement at Trinidad began in about 1861. Although shady ladies certainly worked in town in the city's formative years, the first red-light district in Trinidad grew up very near the Santa Fe Trail behind Commercial Street sometime after 1874. Trinidad's first houses of prostitution were on Mill and Plum Streets, which included many different types of parlor houses. Such places featured better amenities, including dance floors, Saturday night musical trios, and weeknight piano players. The Grand, at Santa Fe and Main Street, even had a swimming pool and Turkish baths! Less expensive accommodations could be found along Main Street, where "bar girls" worked above the local saloons or in restaurants providing curtained booths.

Into this bouquet of sin waltzed Mae (sometimes spelled May) Phelps, probably in about 1885. Very little is known about her early years except that she was born in Maryland between 1856 and 1865 to Irish immigrants. She did spend some time in Pueblo, where in February 1884 she put an advertisement in the *Colorado Daily Chieftain*: "Lost, between Union depot and Front Street, a gold bracelet with a setting of eleven diamonds. $100 reward if returned to Miss May

Phelps, 128 E. Front Street."[1] Front Street was the location of Pueblo's red-light district, and the loss of her valuable bracelet shows that Mae was already very wealthy. By today's calculation, $100 in 1884 would equal around $2,500 today.

Understandably, Mae did not remain in Pueblo for very long. In April a "petition was received from John Arthur and others, stating that Nos. 114, 104, 125 and 122 and other houses on East Front Street are houses of ill fame, detrimental to that part of the city, and asking that the marshal be instructed to order the inhabitants out."[2] Just a month later, a notice of court appearances in the *Chieftain* included "The People versus May Phelps and Lew Hanna." Details were not given, but the one notation—*"scire facias"*—seems to indicate that Mae was required to show proof as to why some judgment against her should not be enforced, or annulled. The notice appeared again in November, this time noting that "May" and Lew were "on forfeited recognizance." Mae had apparently left town, for by December, 128 Front Street was home to G. W. Gill's sewing machine store.[3] As for Mae, she was making her way toward Trinidad.

The city of Trinidad does not appear to have established ordinances against prostitution until about 1891. The new laws proclaimed that law officers could inspect brothels at any time, and that prostitutes were to submit to a monthly health exam. If they were given a clean bill of health, the girls were issued a card to display for officers, health officials, and clients. Still, authorities appeared to be rather lenient when it came to their red-light ladies, especially the madams, and for good reason: With fines, fees, licenses, and exam costs, Trinidad reaped almost 15 percent of its revenue from the red-light district.

Mae does not appear on record in Trinidad until 1891, when she married Edward L. Hess on March 7. Hess was twenty-six years old and Canadian by birth. He had been in Trinidad since at least 1885, when he worked as a druggist and boarded with the family of a prominent local merchant, David Gottlieb. After a brief stint in Leadville in 1890 and 1891, Hess returned to Trinidad in time to marry Mae. Was the marriage one of convenience and the need for a man to deal with the authorities? Perhaps, for more and more young girls were appearing in Trinidad and lending themselves to prostitution's seamier side.

An example was Katie Vidall of Albuquerque, whose sister, Alice, tried to lure her into a bawdy house. Following the death of girls' mother, the sisters had taken respectable jobs at Albuquerque's San Felipe Hotel. Alice left town suddenly, then contacted Katie a few weeks later from a fancy hotel in Trinidad and announced she was dying. Katie rushed to Trinidad, only to find Alice was fine and working at a local brothel. Alice tried to talk her sister into prostitution but, Katie claimed, "I refused, and she called me a fool and left me." Destitute, Katie contacted the town marshal. Donations from some local people netted twenty dollars so Katie could return to Albuquerque and resume respectable employment.[4]

Beginning in 1892, Mae Phelps began appearing in city directories, with and without her new husband. Her residence was always 228 Santa Fe Avenue, an indication of her stability. Although little is known about her brothel, it must have been quite a lavish place. Mae advertised in the *Traveler's Night Guide of Colorado* in 1894 and was sure to take her new girls on "window shopping excursions" in downtown Trinidad for all to see.[5] On at least four occasions, Mae herself had her photograph taken by O. E. Aultman, who made a name for himself photographing much of early Colorado while surveying roads. Her manner of dress in those images illustrates that Mae was well-to-do.

By 1895 Trinidad's red-light district was described as being located on the west end of town, near an area known as Carbon Arroyo. A bridge, romantically nicknamed for the "Bridge of Sighs" in Venice, spanned the arroyo and allowed customers easy access to the district. Bridges above the alleys in back of Trinidad's taverns also allowed customers to access the red-light ladies from an adjoining hillside. Little had changed five years later, when the census identified Mae and Edward Hess both residing at Mae's parlor house, along with ten working girls. Hess was still employed as a druggist, a convenience for the ladies of the house who needed toiletries and medicines.[6]

Some interesting information about Mae's girls can be gleaned from the 1900 census. Their ages ranged from nineteen-year-old Beatrice Wilson to thirty-five-year-old Anna Green. Alice Munroe, Kitty Wright, and Anna Green were married. Alice and Kitty both had children who still lived, while Anna had a child who was no longer alive. Pearl Hopkins, Ethel Russell, and Lilly Evans were all divorced. All of the women were American-born. The presence of prostitutes whose children were not living with them is notable among many of Trinidad's prostitutes, but no clues offer insight as to where those children were. In all, the twenty total prostitutes in Trinidad during 1900 averaged in age between nineteen and fifty-seven. The women had among them a total of thirteen children.

As a reigning madam, Mae Phelps made it clear she that she wasn't afraid of public officials, especially those speaking out of both sides of their mouths. She was not the only one, for most of Trinidad's madams seem to have exhibited little fear of the law. As long as they paid their fines, most of the prostitutes appear to have been left alone. Madams like Mae also worked to assure their girls remained healthy, sending their ill or injured girls to recuperate at the homes of various ranchers for a few weeks.

One of the ranchers, a Mr. Thompson, was once quite embarrassed by a friend who mistook his new bride for a prostitute on the rest. The newlyweds were on their way to the ranch when the acquaintance accosted them and began making some rather inappropriate comments. Thompson was forced to explain to his friend that the lady with him was his wife and also to his new wife that he occasionally had paid the favor of harboring prostitutes who needed a rest. Mrs. Thompson was understandably upset, and it is a credit to Mr. Thompson that he was able to calm her down and remain in the throes of matrimony with her for several years.

The Sanborn fire insurance maps of 1901 show that no fewer than seven brothels existed in Trinidad. Two of them were on Mae's property, one being a smaller crib next door to a much larger, two-story house— the biggest bordello in the district. All of the brothels functioned on six odd-shaped lots directly next door to or across the street from one another. There is no mention in newspapers or other documentation that the girls fought among each other, but Mae surely raked in much of the business. On warm summer nights, it was said, the fire department was occasionally called upon to "rescue" girls from the second floors of their brothels, a feat that required putting ladders up to the windows and watching the girls descend from above. The catch? They weren't wearing underwear. Notably, in 1901 Mae was the only madam with a two-story brothel.

In 1902 Edward Hess died at the young age of thirty-four. He was buried in Trinidad's Masonic Cemetery, but no other information about his death has come forth. How Mae felt about the loss of her husband remains a mystery, as do her activities for the next several years. What is known is that by the time of the 1910 census, there were nine madams in all working in Trinidad. The only woman older than Mae was fifty-eight-year-old Sarah Cunningham. Mae was now forty-five, and the five women working for her were older too. Notably, Anna Green was still with her and was now forty-two. Another woman, Mabel Taylor, was forty-four. There is a chance that Anna and Mabel actually worked as domestics in the house, although the census clearly labels them as prostitutes. Also living there was a Japanese porter named Frank Iwaata. Mae had clearly cut back on the number of her employees and was perhaps suffering financially because of it. But she owned her house, free and clear.

One of four known images of Mae Phelps, taken at the Aultman Studio in Trinidad in 1910.

Courtesy History Colorado, Aultman Collection, #10031331.

Notably, the madams of Trinidad did exhibit wealth from their earnings, power from their association with city and county officials, and generosity from the kindness of their hearts. As one writer put it, "The madams were highly respected, and, well, accepted in terms of standards developed within the economic sector." In about 1910 the madams gathered to create "The Madams' Association," regarded as a "powerful" organization and "carrying with it a significant amount of respect and political influence." The employees of its members "garnered a set fee; the madams deriving a pre-determined percentage."[7]

One of the first duties of the Madams' Association was to establish the "Madam's Trolley System" into the red-light district. Due to the organization's efforts, a new line was built extending to Jansen west of town, allowing miners coming from area coal camps to easily access the red-light district. The Madams' Association successfully presented their case to city officials and even assisted in financing a streetcar bridge as part of the new system. At the time, there were forty-nine shady ladies in Trinidad, a number large enough to merit the trolley system.

How could the city of Trinidad refuse to take the madams' money? They really couldn't, for between April 1911 and March 1912 the city collected nearly $6,000 in fines from the red-light district. By 1912 the number of Trinidad bordellos had grown to twenty-two, with their transient numbers fluctuating on a constant basis. The Madams' Association had the authorities over a barrel, and they knew it. When the city opted to cease using the Madam's Trolley in 1922, eight months before their contract was up, the association sued for breach of contract. But times were changing, and the ladies ultimately settled out of court.

The Madams' Association did have one more goal they wished to accomplish, a most unique idea which the West had never seen: They wanted to establish the Madam's Rest Home, a quiet house outside of town where prostitutes could rest when ill, injured, or pregnant. The chosen spot was a secluded street in the nearby community of Jansen, at the extreme west end of town. Bricks were purchased from the brickyard nearest the red-light district. When finished, the impressive two-story foursquare home featured several bedrooms, a nice porch, and the presence of an ordinary house. From the start, it was made clear that the Madam's Rest Home was to be used exclusively for prostitutes who were ill or "temporarily disabled." While at the home, ladies were strictly forbidden from soliciting or working until they returned to their respective brothels in town.[8]

In his book *Chrysler: The Life and Times of an Automotive Genius*, Vincent Curcio attributes the management of the Madam's Rest Home to "the fabled Jeannetta Kremchek" and claims that former gunslinger L. B. Cutler and "fancy man" Leo Meyer "furnished the home with items . . . salvaged form a string of brothels that had closed in other towns."[9] Jeannetta does not appear on record anywhere near Trinidad. Oddly, neither does Mae Phelps, who was said to have had a hand in establishing the home, which closed in about 1934. Mae does not appear on record in Trinidad at any time after 1912, when she was about fifty-six years old. It is quite possible that the lady finally retired, cashing out her earnings and heading for a place unknown. Wherever she went, Mae made sure she could live out her years in comfort and anonymity, for she seems to have simply disappeared without a trace.

NOTES

---•●•---

Introduction
1. Duffus, *Santa Fe Trail*; Flint and Flint, "Cimarron Cutoff"; "Pioneer Women on the Santa Fe Trail."
2. Lee and Raynesford, *Trails of the Smoky Hill*, 39.
3. Secrest, *Hell's Belles*, 75.
4. Colorado Encyclopedia, "Women in Early Colorado."
5. West, *Saloon on the Rocky Mountain Frontier*, 48.
6. Ibid., 22.
7. Colorado Encyclopedia, "Women in Early Colorado."
8. MacKell, *Brothels, Bordellos & Bad Girls*, 199.
9. Dodds, *What's a Nice Girl*, 16.
10. Blackburn and Richards, "Prostitutes and Gamblers," 241.
11. Dodds, *What's a Nice Girl*, 27.

Sin on the Santa Fe Trail
1. Snow, "Ute Indians." 69.
2. MacKell, *Brothels, Bordellos & Bad Girls*, 107; Reiter, *Women*, 70.
3. MacKell, *Red Light Women*, 94.
4. Duffus, *Santa Fe Trail*.
5. Schuyler Jones, *Hunting and Trading*. 68.
6. Maness, "When Colorado Was Kansas."
7. MacKell, *Red Light Women*, 69; Collins, *Wild Women*, 152.
8. Clavin, *Dodge City*, 267.
9. MacKell, *Red Light Women*, 74.
10. Ibid., 114.

Ladies of the Camps
1. Seagraves, *Soiled Doves*, 23.
2. "Albert D. Richardson's Letters."
3. Brown, *Ghost Towns*, 70.
4. *Golden Weekly Globe*, August 16, 1873, 2.
5. Brown, *Colorado Ghost Towns*, 57.
6. Gilliland, *Summit*, 51.
7. *Breckenridge Bulletin*, May 25, 1907, 1.

8. Sterling, *Oh Be Joyful*, inside cover; Barlow-Perez, *History of Aspen*, 26; Rohrbough, *Aspen*, 201.
9. Wolle, *Stampede to Timberline*, 240.
10. Perry, *I Remember Tin Cup*, 24.
11. Williams, "Creede," 84–85.
12. Wolle, *Stampede to Timberline*, 322.
13. "Reporter Spoke Last Words."
14. Secrest, *Hell's Belles*, 74.
15. Dodds, *What's a Nice Girl*, 27.
16. Peavy and Smith, *Frontier Children*, 98; Ellis, *Life of an Ordinary Woman*, 40.
17. Dodds, *What's a Nice Girl*, 27–28.
18. Gilliland, *Summit*, 69.
19. Ibid., 69; MacKell, *Brothels, Bordellos & Bad Girls*, 30–31, 61, 91.
20. Wolle, *Stampede to Timberline*, 298.

Jane Bowen
1. Peterson, *Over My Dead Body*, 51; *Ninth Census of the United States, 1870*, population schedules; *Aspen Weekly Times*, February 17, 1898, 1.
2. Peterson, *Over My Dead Body*, 51; "Historic Mining Resources"; *Tenth Census of the United States, 1880*.
3. Smith, "The San Juaner," 149–50.
4. Peterson, *Over My Dead Body*, 49.
5. Ibid., 51.
6. Ibid., 49–50.
7. *Silverton Standard*, April 5, 1890, 3.
8. *Silverton Standard*, April 11, 1891, 3.
9. *Silverton Standard*, July 25, 1891, 3; March 5, 1892, 3; and July 30, 1892, 3.
10. *Silverton Standard*, April 6, 1895, 3.
11. *Silverton Standard*, October 21, 1893, 1.
12. Peterson, *Over My Dead Body*, 51–52.
13. National Livestock Association, *Proceedings*, 459.
14. *Aspen Weekly Times*, February 17, 1898, 1.
15. *Silverton Standard*, February 15, 1902, 2; March 1, 1902, 2; and March 8, 1902, 5.
16. Peterson, *Over My Dead Body*, 53.
17. *Silverton Standard*, July 8, 1905, 2.

Mattie Silks
1. Best, *Julia Bulette*, 9.
2. Drago, *Notorious Ladies*, 128–30.
3. MacKell, *Brothels, Bordellos & Bad Girls*, 55.
4. Miller, *Holladay Street*, 72.
5. Secrest, *Hell's Belles*, 215.
6. Ibid., 233, 242.
7. *U.S. IRS Tax Assessment Lists, 1862–1918*, Ancestry.com.
8. Secrest, *Hell's Belles*, 216.

9. *Denver Daily Times,* June 15, 1877, 4.

10. Enss, *Pistol Packin' Madams,* 59.

11. Secrest, *Hell's Belles,* 281.

12. Ibid., 218–19; Parkhill, *Wildest of the West,* 24; Enss, *Pistol Packin' Madams,* 1–6, 58.

13. Harry Drago claims the baby was adopted in 1889, and Chris Enss says Mattie placed the girl, whose name was Rita, in a boarding school. Drago, *Notorious Ladies,* 137; Enss, *Pistol Packin' Madams,* 60.

14. Secrest, *Hell's Belles,* 220.

15. Miller and Mazzulla, *Holladay Street,* 165.

16. *Aspen Daily Times,* January 21, 1890, 4.

17. "Louise L. Thomson," *Washington Marriage Records 1854–2013,* Ancestry.com.

18. Secrest, *Hell's Belles,* 221.

19. MacKell, *Brothels, Bordellos & Bad Girls,* 62; Drago, *Notorious Ladies,* 137.

20. Secrest, *Hell's Belles,* 230–31.

21. Ibid., 120.

22. Ibid., 220; *Colorado Daily Chieftain,* October 12, 1895, 1.

23. *Fort Morgan Times,* April 20, 1900, 5.

24. Ibid.

25. Secrest, *Hell's Belles,* 232.

26. *Durango Democrat,* March 27, 1908, 1.

27. YoExpert, "How did prostitution."

28. Secrest, *Hell's Belles,* 228.

29. Ibid., 266.

30. Ibid., 232–34.

31. Ibid., 223.

Jennie Rogers

1. Ditmer, "City's Last Bordello"; Secrest, *Hell's Belles,* 236.

2. Ibid.

3. Ibid.; Drago, *Notorious Ladies,* 135.

4. Secrest, *Hell's Belles,* 236.

5. An alternate version of this tale is that Jennie simply blackmailed the man by threatening to reveal that he was one of her clients. Parkhill, *Wildest of the West,* 72.

6. Secrest, *Hell's Belles,* 235, 237; Erdoes, *Saloons of the Old West,* 199.

7. Secrest, *Hell's Belles,* 237.

8. MacKell, *Brothels, Bordellos & Bad Girls,* 63; Secrest, *Hell's Belles,* 135, 232.

9. Secrest, *Hell's Belles,* 232.

10. Ibid., 227, 238.

11. Ibid.; *Telluride Daily Journal,* January 7, 1904, 3.

12. Probate for Leah J. Wood, Ancestry.com.

13. Ibid.

14. Ibid.

15. Ibid.

Notes

A Violent Femme

1. Fetter, "Hurdy-Gurdy Gals," 30.
2. Kay Reynolds Blair, *Ladies of the Lamplight*, 91.
3. West, *Saloon on the Rocky Mountain Frontier*, 22.
4. MacKell, *Brothels, Bordellos & Bad Girls*, 92; Eberhart, *Guide to the Colorado Ghost Towns*, 196; Scanlon, *History of Leadville Theater*
5. Author Estelline Bennett wrote of a similar incident in Deadwood that claims the shootout occurred between prostitute Lou Desmond and another shady lady. The bullet struck one of the girls but deflected off her corset. Whether these two events really happened or became a part of one another in the telling is unknown. Bennett, *Old Days of Deadwood*, 112.
6. MacKell, *Brothels, Bordellos & Bad Girls*, 92; Eberhart, *Guide to the Colorado Ghost Towns*, 196.
7. Kay Reynolds Blair, *Ladies of the Lamplight*, 91; Darby Simmons, "Labor of Love," 41.
8. Secrest, *Hell's Belles*, 188–89.
9. Ibid., 206.
10. *Carbonate Chronicle*, February 14, 1880, 5.
11. *Tenth Census of the United States, 1880*; *Carbonate Chronicle*, September 4, 1880, 5; Kay Reynolds Blair, *Ladies of the Lamplight*, 93–94.
12. *Leadville Daily Herald*, November 23, 1880, 4.
13. MacKell, *Brothels, Bordellos & Bad Girls*, 93; Erdoes, *Saloons of the Old West*, 188.
14. Collins, "Mollie May"; Fisher and Holmes, *Gold Rushes and Mining Camps*, 200.
15. *Pueblo Daily Chieftain*, May 12, 1882, 2.
16. Ibid.
17. *Carbonate Chronicle*, June 21, 1884, 7.
18. *Leadville Daily Herald*, August 19, 1884, 4.
19. *Leadville Daily Herald*, March 22, 1884, 4.
20. *Carbonate Chronicle*, August 23, 1884, 5.
21. *Leadville Herald Democrat*, February 28 1886, 2; *Carbonate Chronicle*, March 1, 1886, 4, and March 29, 1886, 8.
22. MacKell, *Brothels, Bordellos & Bad Girls*, 31.
23. *Colorado Daily Chieftain*, April 13, 1887, 6; "Biography: Monheimer"; Collins, "Mollie May."

A Family Affair

1. *Ouray Times*, August 20, 1881, 2.
2. Brown, *Ghost Towns*, 341.
3. "Brothels and Outlaws of the Old West"; Avery, "Itineraries"; Simon, "History of the Vanoli Block," 2–5.
4. Vanoli's Gold Belt Theater and Gold Belt Theater Piano displays, Ouray County Museum, Ouray, Colorado.
5. *Ouray Solid Muldoon*, June 4, 1886, 3.
6. Ibid.; Meador, "Ouray, Colorado," 54. Thesis submitted to the Graduate Faculty of the University of Kansas, December 2, 2010.

7. *Ouray Solid Muldoon*, March 2, 1888, 3.

8. *Colorado Daily Chieftain*, April 3, 1894, 1.

9. *Rocky Mountain Sun*, December 28, 1895, 1.

10. *Telluride Daily Journal*, October 16, 1899, 4.

11. *Ouray Herald*, December 5, 1902, 4; *Plaindealer*, December 12, 1902, 1.

12. *Silverton Standard*, July 30, 1904, 9.

13. *Telluride Journal*, February 1, 1906, 10.

14. Rindfleisch correspondence.

15. *Telluride Journal*, April 27, 1911, 1.

16. *Ouray Plaindealer*, December 15, 1911, 2.

17. *Telluride Daily Journal*, July 7, 1915, 2.

18. *Ouray Herald*, August 13, 1915, 5.

19. Simon, *Teaching with Broken Glass*, 2–5.

20. Ibid.; Gensmer, "Of Painted Women and Patrons," 24.

Laura Bell McDaniel

1. "75 Years Ago." *West Word*, Old Colorado City Historical Society, Colorado Springs, Colorado, May 8, 1888.

2. James M. Horton Probate Record, April 17, 1873, Chariton County Historical Society, Keytesville, Missouri.

3. *Salida Semi-Weekly Mail*, May 20, 1887, courtesy Donna Nevins, Salida, Colorado.

4. Morgan Dunn, Prisoner Record 885, Colorado State Penitentiary, Colorado State Archives.

5. *Salida Semi-Weekly Mail*, May 20, 1887.

6. Ibid.

7. Ibid.

8. *Colorado City Iris*, February 16, 1896, 2.

9. *Twelfth Census of the United States, 1900*.

10. Although Eva Pearl was often referred to as such, she commonly went by her middle name, Pearl. In the 1900 census, she appears at "Pearlie" at the Ursuline Academy. *Liberty (TX) Vindicator*, June 22, 1900, 3.

11. State of Colorado, Division of Vital Statistics, Marriage Record Report for Arthur T. Langdon and Mary Margaret McDaniel, Denver, Colorado; *Colorado, Divorce Index, 1851–1985*, Ancestry.com; Colorado marriage license of Charles Robert Kitto to Pearl Langdon dated July 24, 1912, Denver County Clerk and Recorder, Denver, Colorado.

12. *Colorado Springs Gazette Telegraph*, February 6, 1905, 2.

13. *Colorado Springs Gazette Telegraph*, April 25, 1905, 5.

14. *Colorado City Iris*, February 2, 1906, 2.

15. *Colorado City Iris*, February 9, 1906, 3.

16. *Colorado City Iris*, March 9, 1906, 3.

17. *Colorado City Iris*, March 23, 1906, 3.

18. *Colorado Springs Gazette*, January 21, 1908, 1.

19. *Colorado City Iris*, February 7, 1908, 3.

20. *Colorado City Iris*, April 15, 1909, 1.

21. *Colorado City Iris*, May 7, 1909, 4.
22. Easterbrook, *Time Traveler*, 15.
23. *Colorado City Iris*, July 16, 1909, clippings file, Colorado Springs Public Library, Special Collections.
24. *Colorado City Iris*, February 18, 1910, 1.
25. *Colorado City Iris*, April 15, 1910, 1, and May 27, 1910, 1.
26. *Colorado City Iris*, May 30, 1913, 1.
27. *Colorado City Iris*, June 6, 1913, 1, and August 22, 1913, 3.
28. *State of Colorado v. Laura Bell*, Case #6599, January 1918, El Paso County Courthouse, Colorado Springs, Colorado.
29. Ibid.
30. *Colorado Springs, Colorado City and Manitou City Directory, 1917*; *State of Colorado v. Laura Bell*; Matthews, "Colorado City."
31. Aldridge, "A Peek in the Past."
32. *Record-Journal of Douglas County*, January 25, 1918, 1; *Colorado Springs Independent*, January 31, 1918, 1; *Colorado Springs Gazette Telegraph*, January 20, 1918, clippings file, Penrose Public Library, Special Collections.
33. *Record-Journal of Douglas County*, January 25, 1918, 1.
34. Ibid.
35. Ibid.
36. *Colorado Springs Gazette Telegraph*, January 26, 1918.

Pearl DeVere
1. Minnow, *Pearl DeVere Affair*.
2. *Cripple Creek Times*, June 10, 1897, 1; *Rocky Mountain News*, June 6, 1897, 5; *Denver Republican*, June 6, 1897, 6; *Victor Daily Record*, June 5, 1897, 1.
3. Collins, *Lost Ghost Towns*, 111–12.
4. Secrest, *Hell's Belles*, 226.
5. *Cripple Creek Morning Times*, March 1, 1896, 1.
6. MacKell, *Brothels, Bordellos & Bad Girls*, 165; Alexy Simmons, *Red Light Ladies*, 136–37.
7. When visitor Eleanor Smith toured the Old Homestead in the 1980s, she recalled that the tour guide told the group that Pearl's room may have been the room identified as the ballroom, but a smaller room at the very back of the building was more likely Pearl's boudoir. Today this room appears to have been altered and is probably much smaller than Pearl's original bedroom; given its present dimensions, it could hardly have held all the furnishings listed in Pearl's probate record. Smith interview; Isabelle Martin Probate Case #M-79, El Paso County Courthouse, Colorado Springs, Colorado.
8. Isabelle Martin Probate Case #M-79.
9. *Victor Daily Record*, June 5 1897, 1.
10. *Rocky Mountain News*, June 6, 1897, 5.
11. *Cripple Creek Times*, June 10, 1897, clippings file, Cripple Creek District Museum, Cripple Creek, Colorado.
12. Ibid.

13. Isabelle Martin Probate Case #M-79.
14. Ibid.

French Blanche

1. Blanche must have had a very thick accent, resulting in folks not being able to understand the pronunciation of her last name. Sources vary in the spelling of her name, including LaCoq, Wilcock, LaCraux, LaCrouix, and LaCroug, among others. It is believed, however, that her correct last name was LaCroix. Sally McCready Johnson interview; Teller County Hospital Ledgers.
2. Sally McCready Johnson interview.
3. *American Brewers' Review* 28, July 1914, 517.
4. MacKell, *Brothels, Bordellos & Bad Girls*, 234.
5. Teller County Hospital Ledgers.
6. Ibid.
7. Sally McCready Johnson interview; Keener, "Stories of Some Cripple Creek Personalities," 7–8.
8. Keener, "Stories of Some Cripple Creek Personalities," 7–8.
9. Ibid.
10. Mackin interview.
11. Sally McCready Johnson interview.
12. Waddington correspondence.

Spuds Murphy

1. Dodds, *What's a Nice Girl*, 23.
2. Evans interview, n.d. (tape 7), 45.
3. *Leadville Crystal Carnival*, 19, 31; Edward Blair, *Palace of Ice*, 26.
4. Dodds, *What's a Nice Girl*, 23; Evans interview, November 8, 1952 (tape 9), 90.
5. MacKell, *Brothels, Bordellos & Bad Girls*, 96.
6. Evans interview, May 4, 1951 (tape 4), 9.
7. Ibid.
8. Dodds, *What's a Nice Girl*, 23, 42, 55–56, 58; Benham, "Women in the Colorado State Penitentiary 1873–1916."
9. Evans interview, n.d. (tape 7), 44.
10. Dodds, *What's a Nice Girl*, 56, 62.
11. Ibid., 43, 56, 61–64.
12. Ibid., 61–64.
13. Ibid.
14. Ibid., 64, 66.
15. *Thirteenth Census of the United States, 1910*; Dodds, *What's a Nice Girl*, 68.
16. Dodds, *What's a Nice Girl*, 69.
17. Evans interview, n.d. (tape 7), 43–44.
18. Dodds, *What's a Nice Girl*, 23, 69.
19. Ibid.; "The Congress Hotel, Pueblo, Colorado."
20. Wikibooks, "History of Wyoming."
21. Evans interview, n.d. (tape 7), 45–46.

22. Dodds, *What's a Nice Girl*, 23.
23. Evans interview, n.d. (tape 7), 46.

Laura Evens
1. Fry, *Salida*, 218–19, 232.
2. Laura Evens's name has often been misspelled as "Evans," but most original documentation pertaining to her is spelled "Evens."
3. Evans interview, n.d. (tape 5), 4.
4. Pedro interview, 5.
5. Evans interview, May 4, 1951 (tape 4), 1, 8.
6. Dodds, *What's a Nice Girl*, 22.
7. Evans interview, n.d. (tape 7), 9, 28.
8. Evans interviews, May 4, 1951 (tape 4), 1, 8, and November 8, 1952 (tape 9, side 1), 67, 69.
9. Evans interview, May 4, 1951 (tape 4), 2.
10. Evans interviews, May 4, 1951 (tape 4, 2nd cassette, side 2), 6, 8–9, and May 4, 1951 (tape 4), 1.
11. Dodds, *What's a Nice Girl*, 22.
12. Evans interview, May 4, 1951 (tape 4), 1–2.
13. Ibid, 1–2, 2A–3.
14. Evans interviews, May 4, 1951 (tape 4), 2A–3, and May 4, 1951 (tape 4, 2nd cassette, side 1), 9.
15. Evans interview, May 4, 1951 (tape 4), 7.
16. Evans interview, May 4, 1951 (tape 4, 2nd cassette, side 1), 8–9, and May 4, 1951 (tape 4, 2nd cassette, side 2), 1–2.
17. MacKell, *Brothels, Bordellos & Bad Girls*, 99–100; Fry, *Salida*, 220–21.
18. Evans interview, May 4, 1951 (tape 4), 1, 8.
19. Fisher and Holmes, *Gold Rushes and Mining Camps*, 200.
20. Dodds, *What's a Nice Girl*, 22.
21. Fisher and Holmes, *Gold Rushes and Mining Camps*, 200.
22. Evans interviews, March 12, 1948 (tape 1), 2, and June 8, 1949 (tape 2), 1.
23. Evans interview, June 8, 1949 (tape 3), 1.
24. Secrest, *Hell's Belles*, 107, 219.
25. Evans interview, November 8, 1952 (tape 8), 19–21.
26. MacKell, *Brothels, Bordellos & Bad Girls*, 100.
27. "Lillian Powers of Florence."
28. Evans interview, November 8, 1952 (tape 8), 17.
29. Pedro interview, 6–8.
30. Fry, *Salida*, 220; MacKell, *Brothels, Bordellos & Bad Girls*, 101.
31. Evans interview, March 12, 1948 (tape 1), 1–2.
32. Fisher and Holmes, *Gold Rushes and Mining Camps*, 205.
33. Pedro interview, 13.
34. Fry, *Salida*, 220–21.
35. MacKell, *Brothels, Bordellos & Bad Girls*, 252.
36. Pedro interview, 2, 3, 50–52.

37. Ibid., 8–14.
38. Ibid., 29–31.
39. MacKell, *Brothels, Bordellos & Bad Girls*, 252.
40. "Original Home for the Wurlitzer 30A."
41. Undated newspaper clipping, Laura Evans file, Salida Regional Library, Salida, Colorado.

Bessie Rivers
1. "La Plata County, Coroner Records, 1893–."
2. MacDonald and Arrington, *San Juan Basin*, 118–19.
3. Ibid., 118–20.
4. *Telluride Daily Journal*, June 14, 1904, 3.
5. *Aspen Democrat*, June 19, 1904, 1.
6. *Durango Democrat*, December 27, 1906, 3.
7. Jarvis, *Come on in Dearie*, 25; "Artifact of the Week."
8. "Artifact of the Week"; Jarvis, *Come on in Dearie*, 26–27, 30.
9. Smith, *Sisters in Sin*, 120.
10. Ibid., 121.
11. *Durango Democrat*, February 2, 1908, 1.
12. *Durango Democrat*, March 27, 1908, 1.
13. *Durango Democrat*, May 3, 1908, 2.
14. *Durango Wage Earner*, July 9, 1908, 4, and August 20, 1908, 4; *Durango Democrat*, September 22, 1909, 4.
15. Smith, *Sisters in Sin*, 136.
16. Jarvis, *Come on in Dearie*, 24.
17. Smith, *Sisters in Sin*, 127.
18. *Fourteenth Census of the United States, 1920*; Rivers Family Tree, Ancestry.com; Smith, *Sisters in Sin*, 136.
19. The house survives on the property of the Animas Country Inn. Carlos interview.
20. Smith, *Sisters in Sin*, 135–36.
21. Ibid., 134–35.
22. *Fifteenth Census of the United States, 1930*; Smith, *Sisters in Sin*, 130; Carlos interview; "Frankie Fergason," Find A Grave; Rivers Family Tree, Ancestry.com; Jarvis, *Come on in Dearie*, 31–33.

Lou Bunch
1. Storms, "Madam Lou Bunch Day."
2. Granruth, *Guide to Downtown Central City*, 27.
3. Marshall, "Early Records of Gilpin County," 125, 195.
4. Leslie, Rankin-Sunter, and Wightman, *Central City*, 33.
5. Ibid., 34–36; "James Thomson's Colorado Diary 1872," 113.
6. MacKell, *Brothels, Bordellos & Bad Girls*, 54; Granruth, *Guide to Downtown Central City*, 43.
7. Carter, *Yesterday Was Another Day*, 6.
8. Leslie, Rankin-Sunter, and Wightman, *Central City*, 33.

9. Evans interview, November 8, 1952 (tape 9, side 1), 80; Leslie, Rankin-Sunter, and Wightman, *Central City*, 33.
10. Granruth, *Guide to Downtown Central City*, 44.
11. Linda and Jones, "A Lady Loved by Many," 8.
12. Linda and Jones, "A Lady Loved by Many," 8. ; Carter, *Yesterday Was Another Day*, 5; Denver City Directory for 1892, Ancestry.com; *Rocky Mountain Sun*, June 10, 1893, 2.
13. Evans interview. November 8, 1952 (tape 9, side 1), 67–68, 73–75, 80.
14. Ibid., 68, 77, 81–82.
15. Ibid., 68, 73–75.
16. Ibid., 67–68, 73–75.
17. Jones, "A Lady Loved by Many,"
18. Storms, "Madam Lou Bunch Day"; Pund, "Sporting House Girls."
19. Linda and Jones, "A Lady Loved by Many," 8.
20. Carter, *Yesterday Was Another Day*, 5.
21. Denver City Directory for 1920, Ancestry.com.
22. Evans interview, November 8, 1952 (tape 9, side 1),] 46.
23. Linda and Jones, "A Lady Loved by Many," 8.]; "Louisa Bunch," Find A Grave; "Colo. Madam Gets Grave Marker."

Mae Phelps
1. *Colorado Daily Chieftain*, February 7, 1884, 8.
2. *Colorado Daily Chieftain*, April 22, 1884, 5.
3. *Colorado Daily Chieftain*, May 16, 1884, 8; November 19, 1884, 4 and December 14, 1884, 4.
4. Johnson and Johnson, *Gilded Palaces of Shame*, 32.
5. Secrest, *Hell's Belles*, 227; Dodds, *What's a Nice Girl*, 42.
6. MacKell, *Brothels, Bordellos & Bad Girls*, 113.
7. Donachy, *Larceny and Lace*, 28.
8. Ibid., 28–29.
9. Curcio, *Chrysler*, 86–87.

BIBLIOGRAPHY

———•••———

"Albert D. Richardson's Letters on the Pikes Peak Gold Rush, Written to the Editor of the Lawrence *Republican,* May 22–August 25, 1860." Edited by Louise Barry. From *Kansas Historical Quarterly* 12, no. 1 (February 1943), digitized with permission of Kansas Historical Society. https://www.kshs.org/p/albert-d-rich ardson-s-letters-on-the-pike-s-peak-gold-region/12926.

Aldridge, Dorothy. *A Peek Into the Past.* Colorado Springs, CO: Gowdy-Printcraft Press, 1991.

———. "A Peek in the Past: Soiled Doves, Early-Day Ladies of the Night Assisted Sick and Needy." *Colorado Springs Gazette Telegraph,* January 7, 1984, F21.

"Artifact of the Week." *Talon,* newsletter of the Aztec Museum, Aztec, New Mexico, July 7, 2017. https://www.aztecnews.com/story/2017/07/07/entertainment/ artifact-of-the-week/985.html.

Avery, Karen. "5. Brothels and Outlaws of the Old West," "Itineraries with SW Colo Travel Region." *Ouray Marketing* (blog), February 11, 2008. https://ouraymarketing .blogspot.com/2008/02/itineraries-with-sw-colo-travel-region.html.

Barlow-Perez, Sally. *A History of Aspen.* 2nd ed. Basalt, CO: Who Press, 2000.

Barry, Louise. "The Ranch at Walnut Creek." *Kansas Historical Quarterly* 54 (Summer 1971).

Bauer, William H., James L. Ozment, and John H. Willard. *Colorado Post Offices 1859–1989.* Golden, CO: Colorado Railroad Museum, 1990.

Benham, Marjorie A. "Women in the Colorado State Penitentiary 1873–1916." Master's thesis, University of Colorado at Denver, 1998.

Bennett, Estelline. *Old Days of Deadwood.* Lincoln: University of Nebraska Press, 1982.

Best, Hillyer. *Julia Bulette and Other Red Light Ladies.* Sparks, NV: Western Printing and Publishing Company, 1959.

"Biography: Monheimer." Temple Israel (website). Accessed July 3, 2018. http://www .jewishleadville.org/monheimer.html.

Blackburn, George M., and Sherman L. Richards. "The Prostitutes and Gamblers of Virginia City, Nevada: 1870." *Pacific Historical Review* 48, no. 2 (May 1979).

Blair, Edward. *Palace of Ice: A History of Leadville's Ice Palace 1895–1896.* Colorado Springs, CO: Little London Press, 1972.

Blair, Kay Reynolds. *Ladies of the Lamplight.* Ouray, CO: Western Reflections Publishing, 2002.

BIBLIOGRAPHY

Brown, Robert L. *Colorado Ghost Towns: Past and Present.* Caldwell, Idaho: Caxton Printers, 1981.
———. *Ghost Towns of the Colorado Rockies.* Caxton, ID: Caxton Printers, 1977.
———. *The Great Pikes Peak Gold Rush.* Caldwell, ID: Caxton Press, 1985.
Bunch, Joey. "Denver Street Names Provide a Roadmap Through the Queen City's 154-year History." *Denver Post*, September 23, 2012. http://blogs.denverpost .com/library/2012/09/23/denvers-street-names-provide-roadmap-queen-citys -154year-history/3923.
Carter, Louis J. *Yesterday Was Another Day.* Black Hawk, CO: One Stop Printing & Graphics / St. James Methodist Church, 1989.
Clavin, Tom. *Dodge City: Wyatt Earp, Bat Masterson and the Wickedest Town in the American West.* New York: St. Martin's Press, 2017.
Collins, Jan MacKell. *Lost Ghost Towns of Teller County.* Charleston, SC: History Press, 2016.
———. "Mollie May—Early Sweetheart of Leadville." *Colorado Central Magazine*, November 1, 2014. https://cozine.com/2014-november/mollie-may-early -sweetheart-leadville.
———. *Wild Women of Prescott, Arizona.* Charleston, SC: History Press, 2014.
Cynthia Southern Online, "Madam Lou Bunch Day 2013." Accessed February 8, 2019. http://cynthiasouthern.com/colorado/4-madam-lou-bunch-day-2013.html.
Colorado Encyclopedia. "Women in Early Colorado." Last modified August 9, 2018. https://coloradoencyclopedia.org/article/women-early-colorado.
Colorado General Assembly, House of Representatives. *House Journal of the General Assembly of the State of Colorado.* Berkeley: University of California, 1892.
"Colorado Railroads and Railfanning in 'The Centennial State.'" American-Rails.com. Accessed June 12, 2018. https://www.american-rails.com/co.html.
"The Congress Hotel, Pueblo, Colorado." Pueblo Historical Society. Accessed June 12, 2018. https://www.pueblohistory.org/historic%20photograph%20pages/ congresshotel.html.
Curcio, Vincent. *Chrysler: The Life and Times of an Automotive Genius.* Oxford: Oxford University Press, 2001.
Ditmer, Joanne. "City's Last Bordello Now Glamorous Restaurant." *Denver Post*, April 5, 1999.
Dodds, Joanne West. *What's a Nice Girl Like You Doing in a Place Like This?* Pueblo, CO: Focal Plain, 1996.
Donachy, Patrick L. *Larceny and Lace and Alleged Improprieties.* Vol. 3 of Echoes of Yesteryear series. Trinidad, CO: Inkwell, 1984.
Drago, Harry Sinclair. *Notorious Ladies of the Frontier.* New York: Dodd, Mead, 1969.
Duffus, R. L. *The Santa Fe Trail.* New York: Tudor Publishing, 1936.
Easterbrook, Jim. *The Time Traveler in Old Colorado.* Colorado Springs, CO: Great Western Press, 1985.
Eberhart, Perry. *Guide to the Colorado Ghost Towns and Mining Camps.* 4th ed. Athens, OH: Swallow Press / Ohio University Press, 1981.
Ellis, Anne. *The Life of an Ordinary Woman.* Boston: Mariner Books, 1999.
Englert, Mrs. Kenneth. "Colorado City 1859–1969." Penrose Public Library, Special Collections, Colorado Springs, CO, 978.84.

BIBLIOGRAPHY

Enss, Chris. *Pistol Packin' Madams: True Stories of Notorious Women of the Old West.* Guilford, CT: TwoDot / Globe Pequot Press, 2006.

Erdoes, Richard. *Saloons of the Old West.* Avenel, NJ: Grammercy Books / Random House Value Publishing, 1997.

Fairmount Cemetery. *Distinguished Women Walking Tour.* Denver, CO, n.d.

Fetter, Rosemary. *Colorado's Legendary Lovers: Historic Scandals, Heartthrobs, and Haunting Romances.* Golden, CO: Fulcrum Publishing, 2004.

———. "Hurdy-Gurdy Gals of the Old West." *Colorado Gambler,* June 22–28, 2004.

Find A Grave. http://www.findagrave.com.

Fisher, Vardis, and Opal Laurel Holmes. *Gold Rushes and Mining Camps of the Early American West.* Caldwell, ID: Caxton Printers, 1968.

Flint, Richard, and Shirley Cushing Flint. "Cimarron Cutoff of the Santa Fe Trail." NewMexicoHistory.org. Accessed June 1, 2018. http://newmexicohistory.org/places/cimarron-cutoff-of-the-santa-fe-trail.

Florin, Lambert. *Ghost Town Album.* New York: Superior Publishing, 1962.

Fry, Eleanor. *Salida: The Early Years.* Salida, CO: Arkansas Valley Publishing, 2001.

Gensmer, Kristin A. "Of Painted Women and Patrons: An Analysis of Personal Items and Identity at a Victorian-Era Red Light District in Ouray, Colorado." Master's thesis, Colorado State University, Fort Collins, summer 2012.

Gilliland, Mary Ellen. *Summit: A Gold Rush History of Summit County, Colorado.* Silverthorne, CO: Alpenrose Press, 1980.

Goldfield Historical Society. *Goldfield Historic Walking Tour.* Goldfield, NV, n.d.

Granruth, Alan. *A Guide to Downtown Central City, Colorado.* Black Hawk, CO: One Stop Printing and Graphics, 1989.

Hickman, Roxanne. "Midway Was a Vibrant Settlement." *Gold Rush* (Woodland Park, CO), February 18, 1988. Clippings file, Cripple Creek District Museum, Cripple Creek, CO.

"Historic Mining Resources of San Juan County, Colorado." United States Department of the Interior, National Register of Historic Places, Multiple Property Documentation Form, dated September 27, 2010. http://legacy.historycolorado.org/sites/default/files/files/OAHP/crforms_edumat/pdfs/655.pdf.

"Historic Trianon." The Colorado Springs School. Accessed July 14, 2018. http://www.css.org/about-us/history/historic-trianon.

"Historic Walking Tour Facts." Visit Durango. Accessed June 12, 2018. https://www.durango.org/press-room/fact-sheets/historic-walking-tour-facts.

History.com editors. "Mafia in the United States." Last updated August 21, 2018. https://www.history.com/topics/mafia-in-the-united-states.

"James Thomson's Colorado Diary 1872." Introduction and notes by K. J. Fielding. *Colorado Magazine,* July 1954.

Jarvis, Marion. *Come on in Dearie, or, Prostitutes and Institutes of Early Durango.* Durango, CO: Durango Herald, 1976.

Johnson, Byron A., and Sharon P. Johnson. *Gilded Palaces of Shame: Albuquerque's Redlight Districts 1880–1914.* Albuquerque, NM: Gilded Age Press, 1983.

Jones, Linda. "A Lady Loved by Many." *Colorado Gambler,* December 12, 2011.

Jones, Schuyler, ed. *Hunting and Trading on the Great Plains 1859–1875.* Norman: University of Oklahoma Press, 1986.

Bibliography

Keener, Jim. "Stories of Some Cripple Creek Personalities." Self-published, 2010. Accessed at Cripple Creek District Museum, Cripple Creek, Colorado.

"La Plata County, Coroner Records, 1893–." Transcribed by Kathy Gibson and Julie Pickett. Southwest Colorado Genealogical Society Transcription Project. Last modified January 26, 2016. http://www.swcogen.org/Coroner-Records.html.

La Rocca, Lynda. "The Season of the Spirits at Leadville's Evergreen Cemetery." *Colorado Central*, November 1, 1995. https://cozine.com/1995-november/the -season-of-the-spirits-at-leadvilles-evergreen-cemetery.

"Laura Evans." Salida Regional Library (website). Accessed June 12, 2018. https:// www.salidalibrary.org/laura-evans.

Leadville Crystal Carnival. Leadville, CO: Leadville Crystal Carnival Association, 1896.

Lee, Wayne C., and Howard C. Raynesford. *Trails of the Smoky Hill.* Caxton, ID: Caxton Printers, 1980.

Leslie, Darlene, Kelle Rankin-Sunter, and Deborah Wightman. *Central City, 'The Richest Square Mile on Earth' and The History of Gilpin County.* Black Hawk, CO: TB Publishing, 1990.

Lewis, Jon E. *The West: The Making of the American West.* New York: Carroll & Graf Publishers, 2001.

"Lillian Powers of Florence." Undated newspaper article, Lillian Powers file, Canon City Public Library, Canon City, CO.

Looper, Kitty. *Road to Gold.* Colorado Springs, CO: Little London Press, 1976.

MacDonald, Eleanor D., and John B. Arrington. *The San Juan Basin: My Kingdom Was a County.* Denver, CO: Mido Printing, 1975.

MacKell, Jan. *Brothels, Bordellos & Bad Girls: Prostitution in Colorado, 1860–1930.* Albuquerque: University of New Mexico Press, 2004.

———. *Cripple Creek District: Last of Colorado's Gold Booms.* Charleston, SC: Arcadia Publishing, 2003.

———. *Red Light Women of the Rocky Mountains.* Albuquerque: University of New Mexico Press, 2009.

———. "Trekking Up Hagerman Pass." *Colorado Central*, July 1, 2011. http://cozine .com/2011-july/trekking-up-hagerman-pass.

Maness, Jack. "When Colorado Was Kansas, and the Nation Was (Even More?) Divided." Denver Public Library, Research News, January 26, 2017. https:// history.denverlibrary.org/news/when-colorado-was-kansas-and-nation-was-even -more-divided.

Marshall, Thomas Maitland, ed. "Early Records of Gilpin County, Colorado 1859– 1861." In *University of Colorado Historical Collections*, vol. 2, Mining Series, vol. 1, ed. James F. Willard. Boulder: University of Colorado, 1920.

Matthews, Carl F. "Colorado City, Its Peace Officers; Noted (and Notorious) Characters, Etc.," 1944. Penrose Public Library Special Collections, 36 39.110 Box 5.

Meador, Stephanie R. "Ouray, Colorado: Sense of Place in the Modern Wild West." Master's thesis, University of Kansas, December 2, 2010.

Meyer, Marian. *Mary Donoho: New First Lady of the Santa Fe Trail.* Santa Fe, NM: Ancient City Press, 1991.

Miller, Max. *Holladay Street.* New York: Signet Books, 1962.

Miller, Max, and Fred Mazzulla. *Holladay Street.* New York: Ballantine Books, 1971.

Minnow, Myke. *The Pearl DeVere Affair, 1977.* Cripple Creek District Museum display, Cripple Creek, CO.

Mitchell, Nell. "History of Colorado State Insane Asylum." CMHI Pueblo Museum, October 8, 2016. http://www.cmhipmuseum.org/white-elephant.html.

Moynahan, Jay. *Soiled Doves, Sportin' Women and Other Fallen Flowers.* Spokane, WA: Chickadee Publishing, 2005.

National Livestock Association. *Proceedings of the . . . Annual Convention of the National Live Stock Association: 1900.* Vol. 3. Denver, CO: The Association, 1900.

Noel, Thomas J., and Cathleen M. Norman. *A Pikes Peak Partnership: The Penroses and the Tutts.* Boulder: University Press of Colorado, 2000.

Old Colorado City Walking Tour, Colorado City. Pamphlet in clippings file, Penrose Public Library, Special Collections, Colorado Springs, CO.

Oldach, Denise R. W., ed. *Here Lies Colorado Springs.* Colorado Springs, CO: Fittje Brothers Printing, 1995.

Olivarius-Mcallister, Chase. "Durango's Hidden History of Harlotry." *Durango Herald*, September 24, 2012; updated September 25, 2012. https://durango herald.com/articles/44609.

O'Meara, Walter. *Daughters of the Country: The Women of the Fur Traders and Mountain Men.* New York: Harcourt, Brace & World, 1968.

"Original Home for the Wurlitzer 30A PianOrchestra, Salida, Colorado." Mechanical Music Press. Accessed August 5, 2018. http://www.mechanicalmusicpress.com/ history/pianella/w30a_2_p2.htm.

Parkhill, Forbes. *Wildest of the West.* New York: Holt Publishing, 1951.

Peavy, Linda, and Ursula Smith. *Frontier Children.* Norman: University of Oklahoma Press, 1999.

Perlman, Selig, and Philip Taft. *History of Labor in the United States, 1896–1932.* New York: MacMillan Company, 1935.

Perry, Eleanor. *I Remember Tin Cup.* Littleton, CO: privately published, 1986.

Peterson, Freda Carley. *Over My Dead Body! The Story of Hillside Cemetery.* Norman, OK: Levite of Apache, 1996.

"Pioneer Women on the Santa Fe Trail." Sangres.com. Accessed September 23 2016. http://www.sangres.com/national-trails/santafetrail/womenoftrail01.htm#.XEo GDHdFw2w.

Pund, Jennifer. "Sporting House Girls, Wild Bunch Celebrate Famous Madam." *MMAC Monthly*, June 11, 2016. https://mmacmonthly.com/2016/06/11/sporting -house-girls-wild-bunch-celebrate-famous-madam.

Rawhide, Nevada, postcard from Marius Durand to Josephine Emery, 1908. Accessed July 23, 2018. https://shoppingbin.com/product/1908-rawhide-nevada-nv-busy -downton-street-scene-rppc-ghost-town-bawdy-house/302624651655.

Reiter, Joan Swallow, ed. *The Women.* New York: Time-Life Books, 1978.

BIBLIOGRAPHY

"Reporter Spoke Last Words Over Grave of 'Creede Lily.'" Undated newspaper article, Creede clippings file, Penrose Public Library, Colorado Springs, CO.

Rohrbough, Malcolm. *Aspen: The History of a Silver Mining Town, 1879–1893.* Oxford: Oxford University Press, 1986.

Salida, Colorado, Chamber of Commerce (website). Accessed July 23, 2018. https://salidachamber.org.

Scanlon, Gretchen. *A History of Leadville Theater: Opera Houses, Variety Acts and Burlesque Shows.* Charleston, SC: Arcadia Publishing, 2012. https://books.google .com/books?id=4JZ2CQAAQBAJ&q=Mollie+May#v=snippet&q=Mollie%20 May&f=false.

Seagraves, Anne. *Soiled Doves: Prostitution in the Early West.* Hayden, ID: Wesanne Publications, 1994.

Secrest, Clark. *Hell's Belles: Prostitution, Vice and Crime in Early Denver.* Rev. ed. Boulder: University Press of Colorado, 2002.

"75 Years Ago." *West Word,* newsletter of the Old Colorado City Historical Society, Colorado Springs, CO, May 8, 1988.

"Silverton, Colorado Hillside Cemetery Burial Listings—Letter 'L.'" Accessed June 12, 2018. http://www.silvertonhillside.com/wp-content/uploads/2015/03/ Hillside_L.pdf.

Simmons, Alexy. *Red Light Ladies: Settlement Patterns and Material Culture on the Mining Frontier.* Anthropology Northwest, no. 4. Corvallis: Department of Anthropology, Oregon State University, 1989.

Simmons, Darby G. "Labor of Love: Prostitutes and Civic Engagement in Leadville, Colorado, 1870–1915." Undergraduate honors thesis, University of Colorado, Boulder, spring 2017. https://scholar.colorado.edu/cgi/viewcontent.cgi?article= 2627&context=honr_theses.

Simon, Rebecca. "History of the Vanoli Block," in *Teaching with Broken Glass* (lesson plan), rev. Ouray Archaeology Unit, Colorado State University, n.d. Accessed July 7, 2018. http://www.academia.edu/8070488/Teaching_with_Broken_Glass_ Lesson_Plans.

Smiley, Jerome C. *Semi-Centennial History of Colorado.* Chicago: Lewis, 1913.

Smith, Duane A. "The San Juaner: A Computerized Portrait." *Colorado Magazine* 2, no. 2 (Spring 1975).

———. *Sisters in Sin.* Lake City, CO: Western Reflections Publishing, 2011.

Snow, William M. "Ute Indians and Spanish Slave Trade." *Utah Historical Quarterly* 2 (July 1929).

Sprague, Marshall. *The King of Cripple Creek.* Colorado Springs, CO: Magazine Associates, 1994.

———. *Money Mountain.* Lincoln: University of Nebraska Press, 1953.

———. *Newport in the Rockies.* Chicago: Swallow Press, 1961.

Sterling, Martha Whitcomb. *Oh Be Joyful! An Historic Tale of the Aspen Silver Camp.* Aspen, CO: Roaring Fork Valley Centennial/Bicentennial Committee, 1975.

Storms, Aaron. "Madam Lou Bunch Day Festivities in Central City." *Weekly Register-Call,* June 23, 2016. https://www.weeklyregistercall.com/2016/06/23/madam-lou -bunch-day-festivities-in-central-city.

BIBLIOGRAPHY

"The Story of John Brown." *Desert Gazette* (blog), May 1, 2017. http://desertgazette .com/blog/the-story-of-john-brown.

Thomas, Lowell. *Good Evening Everybody.* Boston: Hall, 1980.

"Travel the Trail: Map Timeline 1873–1878." Santa Fe National Historic Trail, National Park Service. Last updated June 4, 2018. https://www.nps.gov/safe/learn/ historyculture/map-timeline-4.htm.

Traywick, Ben T. *Behind the Red Lights (History of Prostitution in Tombstone).* Tombstone, AZ: Red Marie's, 1993.

Twitty, Eric. *Historical Context: Interstate 70 Mountain Corridor.* Prepared by Mountain States Historical and CH2M HILL for the Colorado Department of Transportation, June 2014.

Warman, Cy. *Frontier Stories: "A Quiet Day In Creed."* New York: Charles Scribner's Sons, 1898.

West, Elliott. *The Saloon on the Rocky Mountain Frontier.* Lincoln: University of Nebraska Press, 1979.

Wikibooks. "History of Wyoming/Modern Wyoming, 1890–1945." Last modified October 23, 2018, 10:35. https://en.wikibooks.org/wiki/History_of_Wyoming/ Modern_Wyoming,_1890-1945.

Wikipedia. "Helen Ring Robinson." Last modified September 24, 2018, 19:28. https://en.wikipedia.org/wiki/Helen_Ring_Robinson.

Wiles, Gary, and Delores Brown. *Femme Fatales, Gamblers, Yankees and Rebels in the Gold Fields (1859–1869).* Hemet, CA: Birth of America Books, 2005.

Williams, Albert, Jr. "Creede, A New Mining Camp." In *The Engineering Magazine,* vol. 3. New York: McGraw Hill Publishing, 1892.

Wolle, Muriel Sibell. *Stampede to Timberline.* Boulder: Muriel Sibelle Wolle / University of Colorado, 1949.

YoExpert. "How did prostitution in Denver, Colorado come to an end?" Accessed August 5, 2018. http://american-history.yoexpert.com/social-history-6843/how -did-prostitution-in-denver-colorado-come-to-an-2365.html.

"Yuma County Pioneers: Mattie Silks (Martha Thomson–Martha Ready)." Yuma County, Colorado (website). Accessed June 6, 2018. http://www.cogenweb.com/ yuma/photos/pioneer/wray/MattieSilks.htm.

Ancestry.com

Chaffee County Assessment Roll, 1884, Buena Vista, Colorado.

City directories for Colorado and Kansas, *U.S. City Directories, 1822–1995.*

Civil War Records.

Colorado, County Marriage Records and State Index, 1862–2006.

Colorado, Divorce Index, 1851–1985.

"Colorado—Regular Revenue, Vol. 9, 1892," *U.S. IRS Tax Assessment Lists, 1862– 1918.*

Colorado, Wills and Probate Records, 1875–1974.

Denver City Directories for 1892, 1906, 1915, 1916, 1917, and 1920, *U.S. City Directories, 1822–1995.*

Durango, Colorado, City Directory for 1911, *U.S. City Directories, 1822–1995.*

BIBLIOGRAPHY

1880 U.S. Census Index.
Headstones Provided for Deceased Union Civil War Veterans, 1861–1904.
Indiana, Marriage Index, 1800–1941.
Iowa, State Census Collection, 1836–1925.
"Laura Bell McDaniel," It Must Be My Side of the Tree Family Tree.
"Bessie Rivers," Rivers Family Tree.
"Laura Turner," Winstongen Family Tree.
"Leah J. 'Jennie' Tehme Rogers," Jennie Rogers Family Tree.
Philbrick-Reid-Lutz-Johanson-S Family Tree.
Probate for Leah J. Wood, Case #12912, October 29, 1909. *Colorado, Wills and Probate Records, 1875–1974.*
Pueblo City Directory for 1906, *U.S. City Directories for 1822–1995.*
Washington, Marriage Records 1865–2004.
U.S. City Directories, 1822–1995.
U.S., Civil War Draft Registration Records, 1863–1865, Missouri 6th Congressional District, vol. 3 of 3.
U.S. IRS Tax Assessment Lists, 1862–1918.
U.S. Passport Applications, 1795–1925.

Census Records
Seventh Census of the United States, 1850. National Archives Microfilm Publication M432, 1009 rolls.
Ninth Census of the United States, 1870. National Archives Microfilm Publication M593, 1,761 rolls.
Tenth Census of the United States, 1880. National Archives Microfilm Publication T9, 1,454 rolls.
Schedules of the Colorado State Census, 1885. National Archives Microfilm Publication M158, 8 rolls.
Twelfth Census of the United States, 1900. National Archives Microfilm Publication T623, 1,854 rolls.
Thirteenth Census of the United States, 1910. National Archives Microfilm Publication T624, 1,178 rolls.
Fourteenth Census of the United States, 1920. National Archives Microfilm Publication T625, 2076 rolls.
Fifteenth Census of the United States, 1930. National Archives Microfilm Publication T626, 2,667 rolls.
Sixteenth Census of the United States, 1940. National Archives Microfilm Publication T627, 4,643 rolls.

City Directories
Directory of Colorado Springs, Manitou Springs and Colorado City for 1888. Colorado Springs, CO: S. N. Francis, 1888.
Directory of Colorado Springs, Manitou Springs and Colorado City for 1890. Colorado Springs, CO: S. N. Francis, 1890.
Directory of Colorado Springs, Colorado City and Manitou, 1894. Colorado Springs, CO: Gazette Printing Company, 1894.

BIBLIOGRAPHY

Official Directory of Colorado City and Manitou, 1899. Colorado Springs, CO: Tourist Publishing Company, 1899.

City Directory of Colorado Springs, Colorado City and Manitou Springs, 1900. Colorado Springs, CO: Giles Directory Company, 1900.

City Directory of Colorado Springs, Colorado City and Manitou Springs, 1901. Colorado Springs, CO: Giles Directory Company, 1901.

City Directory of Colorado Springs, Colorado City and Manitou for 1902. Colorado Springs, CO: Giles Directory Company, 1902.

City Directory of Colorado Springs, Colorado City and Manitou, 1903. Colorado Springs, CO: Giles Directory Company, 1903.

Colorado Springs, Colorado City and Manitou City Directory, 1904–1905. Colorado Springs, CO: R. L. Polk & Co., 1904.

Colorado Springs, Colorado City and Manitou City Directory, 1905–06. Colorado Springs, CO: R. L. Polk & Co, 1905.

Colorado Springs, Colorado City and Manitou City Directory, 1907–08. Colorado Springs, CO: R. L. Polk & Co, 1907.

Colorado Springs, Colorado City and Manitou City Directory, 1908. Colorado Springs, CO: R. L. Polk & Co., 1908.

Colorado Springs, Colorado City and Manitou, 1909. Colorado Springs, CO: R. L. Polk & Co., 1909.

Colorado Springs, Colorado City and Manitou, 1910. Colorado Springs, CO: R. L. Polk & Co., 1910.

Colorado Springs, Colorado City and Manitou City Directory, 1912 (Colorado Springs, CO: R. L. Polk Directory Company, 1912.

Colorado Springs, Colorado City and Manitou City Directory, 1914. Colorado Springs, CO: R. L. Polk Directory Company, 1914.

Colorado Springs, Colorado City and Manitou City Directory, 1916. Colorado Springs, CO: R. L. Polk Directory Company, 1916.

Colorado Springs, Colorado City and Manitou City Directory, 1917. Colorado Springs, CO: R. L. Polk, 1917.

A Complete City Directory of Cripple Creek, Victor, and the Towns of the Cripple Creek Mining District, 1896. Denver, CO: Gazetteer Publishing Company, 1896.

Cripple Creek District Directory, 1905. Denver, CO: Gazetteer Publishing Company, 1905.

Cripple Creek District Directory, 1907. Denver, CO: Gazetteer Publishing Co., 1907.

Cripple Creek District Directory, 1917–18, vol. 10. Denver, CO: Gazetteer Publishing Co, 1917.

Correspondence with Author

Drake, Ray. Cripple Creek, Colorado. September 2012.

Lawson, Rose Mary. Chariton County Historical Society, Keytesville, Missouri. September 17, 2011.

Oldach, Denise. Colorado Springs, Colorado. February 1, 1995.

Rindfleisch, George. Ouray, Colorado. May 6, 2015.

Waddington, Paula Johnson. Delta, Colorado. May 12, 2012, and July 23, 2018.

BIBLIOGRAPHY

Documents

Chaffee County Marriage Records. Clerk and Recorder, Chaffee County Courthouse, Buena Vista, Colorado.

"Colorado Springs Council Proceedings and Reports, April 6, 1917." El Paso County Courthouse, Colorado Springs, Colorado.

Colorado Springs property records, El Paso County Assessor's Office, Colorado Springs, Colorado.

El Paso County Marriage and Divorce Records. El Paso County Courthouse, Colorado Springs, Colorado.

Estate of Laura Bell McDaniel, Probate File #M311. El Paso County Courthouse, Colorado Springs, Colorado.

Fairview Cemetery Records. Fairview Cemetery Sexton's Office, Fairview Cemetery, Colorado Springs, Colorado.

Missouri Marriage Records of Saline County, Missouri. Volume IV, book D, 1874–1881.

Sanborn Insurance Company. Sanborn Map for Colorado City, Colorado, November 1902.

———. Sanborn Map for Cripple Creek, Colorado, December 1894.

———. Sanborn Map for Trinidad, Colorado, 1901.

State of Colorado, Bureau of Vital Statistics, Denver Public Library.

Teller County Grantor/Grantee Ledgers. Teller County Clerk and Recorder, Teller County Courthouse, Cripple Creek, Colorado.

Teller County Hospital Ledgers. Cripple Creek District Museum, Cripple Creek, Colorado.

Teller County Tax Records for 1904. Teller County Treasurer's Office, Teller County Courthouse, Cripple Creek, Colorado.

Interviews

Buss, Richard "Red." Colorado City, Colorado. Interview with author, 1989.

Carlos, Andres "Pablo." Animas Museum, Durango, Colorado. Interview with author, August 1, 2018.

Dymkoski, Catherine H. Great-granddaughter of Jacob Schmidt. Interview with author, winter 2018.

Evans, Laura. Transcripts of interviews by Fred Mazzulla, March 12, 1948–January 20, 1954 (11 tapes). History Colorado, Denver, courtesy of Salida Regional Library, Salida, Colorado. https://www.salidalibrary.org/laura-evans.

Hern, Lodi. Old Homestead House Museum, Cripple Creek, Colorado. Interviews with author, 1998–2012.

Johnson, Richard. President of the Board, Cripple Creek District Museum, Cripple Creek, Colorado. Interviews with author, 1998–2003.

Johnson, Sally McCready. Cripple Creek, Colorado. Interview with author, March 1996.

Mackin, Steve. Cripple Creek, Colorado. Interview with author, 2010.

Pedro, Fern. Transcript of interview regarding Laura Evans by Fred Mazzulla, January 20, 1954 (tape 10). History Center, Denver, courtesy of Salida Regional Library, Salida, Colorado. https://www.salidalibrary.org/laura-evans.

Smith, Eleanor. Los Osos, California. Interview with author, May 2003.

Bibliography

Newspapers
Aspen (CO) Democrat
Aspen (CO) Weekly Times
Breckenridge (CO) Bulletin
Carbonate Chronicle (Leadville, CO)
Colorado City (CO) Argus
Colorado City (CO) Independent
Colorado City (CO) *Iris*
Colorado Daily Chieftain (Pueblo, CO)
Colorado Springs (CO) Gazette
Colorado Springs (CO) Gazette Telegraph
Colorado Springs (CO) Independent
Colorado Springs (CO) Weekly Gazette
Cripple Creek (CO) Morning Times
Cripple Creek (CO) Times
Denver Daily Times
Denver Republican
Durango (CO) Daily Journal
Durango (CO) Democrat
Durango (CO) Wage Earner
Fort Morgan (CO) Times
Golden (CO) Weekly Globe
Leadville (CO) Daily Herald
Leadville (CO) Democrat
Leadville (CO) Herald Democrat
Leadville (CO) Weekly Herald
Liberty (TX) Vindicator
Ouray (CO) Herald
Ouray (CO) Solid Muldoon
Ouray (CO) Times
Plaindealer (Ouray, CO)
Pueblo (CO) Daily Chieftain
Record-Journal of Douglas County (Castle Rock, CO)
Rocky Mountain News (Denver, CO)
Rocky Mountain Sun (Aspen, CO)
Salida (CO) Semi-Weekly Mail
San Miguel (CO) Examiner
Silverton (CO) Standard
Telluride (CO) Daily Journal
Telluride (CO) Journal
Victor (CO) Daily Record
Wray (CO) Rattler

INDEX

Index

INDEX

INDEX

INDEX

INDEX

Warmoth, John, 69
Warmoth Moats Hooyer, Birdie May, 69,
    70, 74, 76–77, 81
Warner, Blanche, 107
Warner, Marsh, 48
Warner, Stanley C., 48
Warwick, Della (Lizzie), 134
Warwick, Nel, 135
Washington, Hazel, 137
Washington, Lillie, 137
water fights, 30
Watson, Sarah, 75
Watt, John, 79
Weeks, Freddie, 95
Weil, J. L., 87, 91
Weis, Jose, 2
Wellington, Ella, 43, 44
Wellington, Mayme, 90
Wellington Mine, 10
Westminster Hall, 20, 21
Weston, Fay, 116
Weston Terrace, 116
White, Laura, 75
White, Mable, 90
Wilcock Denny, Katherine [Dora],
    97–98, 101–2
Wilson, Beatrice, 142

Wilson, Hi, 14
Winds, Annie, 56
Womack, Bob, 86
women, respectable
    brothels as domestic abuse shelters
      for, 119
    early scarcity of, x–xi, 8–9
    friendships with, 54
    prostitute aspirations, xv, 16
    rehabilitation agendas of, xi
    Santa Fe Trail travel, ix, 1
Wood, John "Jack," 43, 44, 48
Wood, Leah J. (Jennie Rogers), 29–30,
    36, 40–48, *45*
Woods, Mattie, 30
Wootten, Richard "Uncle Dick," 1
workplace locations. *See also* brothels
    and bordellos; parlor houses
    along Santa Fe Trail, 3
    at mining camps, xv, 26, 49
    service charge comparisons, xvi
    in towns and cities, 25–26, 59, 61
Worling, Dolly, 78
Wright, Kitty, 142
Wright, Madam, 132

Young, May, 137

ABOUT THE AUTHOR

---•●•---

Jan MacKell Collins has been a published author, speaker, and presenter since 2003. Her focus has always been on western history, with an emphasis on historical prostitution. Collins has published numerous articles on her subjects in such magazines as *True West, Montana Magazine, All About History,* and many regional magazines. She currently resides in Oregon, where she continues researching the history of prostitution.